POET IN NEW YORK

Poet in New York

by *FEDERICO GARCIA LORCA*

e.1

Complete Spanish Text
with A New Translation
b y BEN BELITT

GROVE PRESS, INC.
New York

861
GARCIA LORCA

Spanish Text copyright © 1940 by Francisco García Lorca

This English translation copyright © 1955 by Ben Belitt

Introduction copyright © 1955 by Angel del Río

Library of Congress Catalog Card Number 55-5108

First Grove Press Edition 1955

Thirteenth printing

Manufactured in the United States of America

TABLE OF CONTENTS

vi

INTRODUCTION

POET IN NEW YORK: TWENTY-FIVE YEARS AFTER

It has been said repeatedly that *Poet in New York* is the most enigmatic and challenging of Lorca's works. When the poems were first circulated, either by publication in periodicals or, as was customary with Lorca, through readings to friends, few could see a clear connection in theme, language, imagery or tone with what was considered typical of the author's poetic world, deeply rooted in the Spanish tradition and landscape. It was the opinion of many that Lorca, by abandoning his usual sources of inspiration, had gone astray. Some spoke of artificiality and considered these poems merely a momentary diversion. The strangeness of the book was taken in some quarters as an attempt by Lorca to escape his wide fame as a purely popular poet; in others, it was attributed to his desire to compete with other Spanish poets, especially Rafael Alberti, who at the moment had set out on the surrealist adventure.

The work in its entirety was not published until 1940. By then the situation had changed considerably: surrealism had been accepted as an expression of the time's restlessness. Moreover, the tragic death of the poet, the defeat of the Spanish Republic and the shadow of war extending over the planet conditioned critic and reader alike to see in these turbulent pieces something more than a meaningless jabber. José Bergamín, in his preface to the Séneca edition, as well as Juan Larrea, in a later commentary, clearly pointed out the prophetic quality of the book. Both of them spoke for the dismal attitude of the Spanish exiles.

But it was probably not until the appearance of the book in English, later in the same year, in the excellent translation of Rolfe Humphries, that the true meaning of Lorca's vision, together with its high poetic quality, began to be recognized. Conrad Aiken, reviewing the book for the *New Republic,* grasped Lorca's message clearly, together with his magnificent 'prodigality of image' and the purity of his indignation towards an America which had forgotten Heaven. He saw a warning in

> the recurring preoccupation of this book—pain, pain and suffering, fear of death and injury, the agony of the conscious mind in the presence of universal pain . . . There has been no more terribly acute critic of America than this steel-conscious and death-conscious Spaniard, with his curious passion for the modernities of nickel and tinfoil and nitre, and for the eternities of the desert and the moon. He hated us, and rightly, for the right reasons.

Other critics like R. W. Short, Eugene Jolas, John Gould Fletcher and Dudley Fitts similarly welcomed the book as both a major work and a significant poetic view of the less attractive features of the North American metropolis.

Yet, in the Hispanic world, among those who have followed Lorca's progress as an artist and for whom he was one of the best in a galaxy of contemporary Spanish-speaking poets unsurpassed perhaps in the literature of Europe (a fact unfortunately little known and never recognized), this book was often dismissed as an extemporaneous flight into alien areas, not to be considered in the main stream of his poetic development. It is still the mistaken view not only of Spanish but of some English and North American critics, such as Roy Campbell and John A. Crow.

The reasons for this are apparent. Lorca speaks here with a new voice. The pessimism, the undercurrent of social or rather human protest in face of what can be called the dehumanization of modern man and life, did not fit into the conventional image of a folkloric poet which had been created after the great success of the *Gypsy Ballads*. Even with respect to language, the differences from the previous works were striking. Color was not lacking; but the greens and reds, the yellow, the saffron, the olive and carnation hues were now replaced by ashes, grays, dry lemon or coal black. Imagery and metaphor, ruled by seeming incoherence, appeared in the light of an exercise in surrealism.

It may be useful in this connection to point out that once we have rejected the stereotype of Lorca as a mere Andalusian and Spanish poet, this book may not be as unrelated to the rest of his work as it appears to be at a superficial glance. Endowed as few poets have been with the grace and genius of Poetry, he had the capacity—one could almost say the necessity—of transforming every impression, everything that went through his senses, into poetry. It has become clear with the passing of years that there are *many* Lorcas; or, to put it in another way, there are many keys in the wide gamut of his work.

It should not be overlooked that, from the first childlike and ingratiating lyrics of his youth, there is a bitter root (*raiz amarga*). At its most revealing level, we find in Lorca a spirit obsessed with primitive passion, with earthy emotion and, above all, with a vision of death—his great and all-embracing theme. As his distinguished countryman Pedro Salinas has said, "The poetic kingdom of Lorca, full of forebodings, threats and omens is under the rule of a unique and unchallenged power: Death." Furthermore, all his theater, and a great part of his poetry, underneath the brilliance of a dazzling sensory rendering of matter, from the infinitesimal to the cosmic, breathes a sense of dissatisfaction and sterility: the sacrifice of Mariana Pineda, the hopeless longing of Doña Rosita, the inexorable fate of his gypsies or of the lovers in *Blood Wedding*, the tragicomic loving of Don Perlimplín, or the self-destroying fury of Bernarda Alba. Everywhere the work is moved by mysterious forces impeding human fulfillment.

In this light, *Poet in New York*, rather than appearing a whimsical, eccentric exercise in a realm alien to the poet, gains significance as a foreseeable reaction to the shock of a reality crucially different from his own. The City becomes a powerful symbol of this universal unfulfillment. Without denying the obscurity of many of his lines, or what may seem the wilful abandonment of his sensibility, we can see in this book a troubling revelation of the disrupting forces of the modern world in the mesh of steel and misery that he saw in New York. At the same time, the book can be viewed as a clear link between his early and later works—deeper, more dramatic, in substance and style, and an important step in his artistic development. It came immediately after Lorca had deviated from the dominant folkloric and traditional elements to explore, in the "Ode to Salvador Dali" and his "Ode to the Most Blessed Sacrament," a type of poetry characterized by an intellectual consciousness which Spanish criticism may have woefully underestimated.

However much he may have been rooted in the soil of Spanish tradition, with its richness of popular elements, Lorca was far more than a local poet. He was, above all, a *natural* poet, a poet incarnate with a godlike, or perhaps demonic, impulse to re-create in word and image the world of reality.

2.

Everything indicates that the New York poems are the result of an authentic artistic and personal experience which, as in all true poets, transcends the purely personal. The United States was the first foreign land visited by García Lorca. It is not clear why he came to New York instead of going to Paris, London, Rome, Berlin, as was usual among Spanish artists and intellectuals during those years characterized by a strong current of "Europeanization" under the influence of Ortega y Gasset. There was, of course, a favorable coincidence: the trip to the United States of Lorca's great friend and mentor Professor Fernando de los Ríos. But those inclined to interpret the hidden forces which guide the fate of poets may read something of an omen into the coming of Lorca to this—for him— completely remote world.

Biographers have spoken of the urgent need felt by the poet to get away from his natural medium, unsatisfied as he was by the great and popular success of his *Gypsy Ballads,* which had placed him in a not altogether favorable light in the coterie of new poets in Spain. A trip to Paris, in the pattern of many of his countrymen, could not satisfy his desire to retire from the limelight. He grasped the opportunity offered by the trip of his friend De los Ríos, for an entirely complete change of atmosphere. Thus his journey to New York could be interpreted as a flight, and the book, although quite dissimilar in purpose and language, could be compared, as in fact it frequently has been, with Rimbaud's *Une Saison en Enfer.*

Whatever the immediate motives of the poet's sojourn in New York, these poems will have coherence and meaning only if we consider them as the outcome of a triple crisis: an emotional crisis in the life of the poet, to which he constantly alluded in those days without completely revealing its nature; a crisis coincident with, and, in part, a result of, the crisis through which all modern poetry was going with the advent of surrealism and other "isms"; and finally, a crisis—a profound one—in the American scene that the poet was going to encounter.

Sometimes it is forgotten that what Lorca found on coming to these shores was the dismal New York of 1929 and 1930, of the Depression, with all the shabby disarrangement accompanied by a mood of pessimism and despair. He probably did not realize what it all meant, ignorant as he was of economic laws and history, but the signs and portents were there for him to perceive and express in an incoherent and semiconscious way. If we bear this in mind, it is not difficult to understand how the loneliness that he brought within him found a perfect counterpart in the disruption and lack of direction that the reality of the city forced upon him. It could be said that the poet found himself in New York, or at least that he discovered here some new levels of his innermost personality. It is, therefore, not strange that the dreamlike symbols of doom and suffering grope everywhere in these poems.

For some persons who met the poet during his year in New York this was not always clear. Thus, Professor John Crow, a Columbia student at the time, who lived in the same dormitory and saw the poet frequently, seems to think that the entire book, which he considers "Lorca's poorer poetry," is false and in great part senseless. It is his belief that the anguish was simply a result of the isolation and confusion of the poet in a new atmosphere which he never really understood:

I came in intimate contact with Lorca day after day [he says] while he was work-ing on the *Poeta en Nueva York*, and if he was experiencing any "mortal anguish," I am a monkey's uncle. At times he must have felt very lonely, but at other times he drank, necked, and caroused like many another young masculine animal, and seemed to have a rather hilarious time doing it. When he settled down to write poetry in the early morning hours of New York after midnight, it was with the strained voice, the high key, the midnight fervours of nostalgia burning deep in the darkness. And the picture was no salutary sight.

Crow, well-meaning, was misled by the overwhelming vitality of Lorca. Federico was, above all, what the Spanish çall "simpático"— playful, full of humor, almost histrionic in his gaiety, an extraordinary creature who made friends easily. This was the light in his character; but there was also a shadow which, in his human relationships, he probably showed only to those who knew him intimately. The writer of these lines, a friend of the poet since his earliest days in Madrid, saw him also day by day during his stay in New York, and his impression was quite different. Lorca played, talked, laughed, made jokes about everything and everybody, but the anguish was a real one, as were also the personal gloom and emotional preoccupations which he lived through during these months. The sources of this emotional crisis are obscure, at least for those who knew him superficially. They touch delicate fibers of his personality, problems which cannot be hastily appraised or dismissed, but which left a very real impact on the book; so that only when they are taken into consideration can the work, or at least some parts of it, be understood in all its significance.

To be sure, there was nothing very eventful in his life in New York. He arrived about the latter part of June or early in July of 1929 and went immediately to live on one of the top floors of John Jay Hall, in a room which he kept until his departure in the spring of the following year. At the beginning he pretended to have come to study and registered in a class of English for foreigners. He withdrew after the first week, convinced of his incapacity for learning a foreign language. The only thing he learned in that week was how to mimic the accent and gestures of his teacher and fellow-students—Chinese, Persians, Roumanians. During the summer almost his only contacts were with a few Spanish friends, and for several evenings he taught folk songs to Spanish students.

At the end of the Summer Session the group dispersed, and Federico, as we always called him, went to Vermont to visit an American friend. This was a fellow-poet, according to him, a Mr. Cummings, whom he had met a few months before in the Residencia at Madrid. This friend, I regret to say, I have never been able to identify; and if he was indeed a poet he would have been Lorca's only contact with an American creative writer during his stay in this country. Typical of Lorca's reaction to the new atmosphere was the panic, half simulated and half in earnest, that possessed the traveler on entering the bustle of Grand Central. On boarding the train, he was genuinely worried by his removal from all means of communication, for he could not speak a word of English. He dramatized the incident by shouts and gestures and was not at ease until the friend who had taken him to the train assured him, after talking with the conductor, that he would be left safely at his destination. In Vermont, where he stayed but a few days, he wrote, or at least conceived, the two poems dated at Eden Mills.

From there he went to a modest farm in the Catskills near Shandaken, where I was spending my vacation. His arrival there was no less typical of his relationship with American life than had been his departure for Vermont. Knowing his incapacity for coping with all practical matters, I wrote him detailed instructions: he must wire me the time of arrival in Kingston; in case I were not there, he must take a bus to Shandaken. The day we were waiting for him no telegram came and there was no sign of Lorca. We began to be worried lest he might be lost, when at nightfall we saw a taxi chugging along the dirt road of the farm. The driver wore an expression of resigned ferocity, and Federico, half out of the window, on seeing me, began to shout in a mixture of terror and amusement. What had happened, of course, was that Lorca, finding himself alone in Kingston, had decided to take a taxi without being able to give the right directions to the driver. They had been going around mountain roads until a kindly neighbor had given them our address. The fare was $15. As Lorca had spent all his money, I had to pay the driver and placate his fury. Federico's terror was the outcome of his conviction that he was lost, without money enough to take care of the bill. Immediately he gave the incident a fantastic twist and said that the driver, whom he could not understand, had tried to rob and kill him in a dark corner of the woods.

At the farm, he spent part of his time writing. He also read to us, in addition to his new poems, the play *Don Perlimplín,* which he had revised in New York, and fragments of *The Shoemaker's Prodigious Wife, When Five Years Passed* and *The Public*—the last two of a surrealist character with themes and language close to those of *Poet in New York.* He spent many hours with the farmer's two children—the 'boy Stanton' of the poem which bears his name and a girl who inspired his "Girl Drowned in a Well." How he communicated with the children was a miracle of inventiveness. They were fascinated by Federico, especially when he sang or improvised folk songs on a dilapidated and out-of-tune piano or when he told them stories in an incredible Spanish, often acting the parts of the characters and dramatizing the action. From Shandaken he went for the rest of the vacation to the house of Professor Federico de Onís near Newburgh.

When classes resumed at Columbia, he came back to the city. The fall and winter were passed in very much the same way as the earlier days of the summer after he arrived. He walked constantly through the city: in Harlem, on the Battery, the Lower East Side, or Broadway and Fifth Avenue. He frequently visited the zoo and went to movies or musical comedies. He made some acquaintances among people who spoke Spanish. But his constant companions were a group of Spaniards, most of whom he had known for many years. Beside Professor de Onís and myself were the poet León Felipe, translator of Whitman; Dámaso Alonso, today one of the leading critics and scholars of Spain and also a poet of importance; the painter Gabriel García Maroto, who in 1921 had published Lorca's *Book of Poems,* his first work of some consequence; and José Antonio Rubio Sacristán, a close friend and fellow-resident at the Residencia de Estudiantes in Madrid, who at the time was in the United States studying economics. Occasionally the group was augmented by Professor Augusto Centeno, of Princeton, and Andrés Segovia. Later on Lorca was frequently seen with the dancer Argentinita—whom he had known well since 1920, when she had danced in the earliest Lorca dramatic venture, *The Evil Doing of the Butterfly*—and with Ignacio Sánchez Mejías, the bullfighter to whom Lorca was to dedicate, years later, one of his greatest works and one of the most moving elegies of contemporary poetry.

Of Americans, with the exception of a small group of fellow-residents in John Jay Hall with whom he often met and went around, he came to know well only two: the critics Herschel Brickell and Mildred Adams, both of whom were interested in Hispanic art and literature. With these exceptions, he did not get so much as a glimpse of New York literary life.

In the spring of 1930 he was invited to lecture in Cuba, and he left the United States, still without having learned a word of English and pronouncing with Spanish phonetics the few he was forced to use, saying, for instance, "Ay go to Teemes Esquaare."

All this, normal and trivial as it might seem, is nevertheless meaningful, we believe, for it clearly shows that whatever significance *Poet in New York* may have does not spring from any genuine contact with actual American life, which the poet saw only from the outside, nor from any intimate knowledge of American thought and literary currents. But it does not follow that we have therefore to repudiate his poetic vision. For the true poet is a "seer" in more than the literal sense of the word, and he usually deals with a special type of reality, of which the external signs are at best mere points of reference, to be reconceived in his imagination and to be organized according to a special system of symbols and a peculiar vision that the poet creates.

In his tireless ramblings Lorca gathered impressions, which in his vigils he distilled into verse. It is not pure coincidence that the first poem bears the title of "Back From a Walk," nor should we be surprised at the nocturnal character and inspiration of many other poems. The book was created very slowly and never assumed a final form satisfactory to the author, since he left it unpublished. While here, he probably wrote few poems. I remember, among the first ones, the ode to "The King of Harlem" and "Brooklyn Bridge Nocturne," and during the Catskill days, "Nocturne of the Void" and "Ruin." My recollection after twenty-five years is somewhat hazy, but although the essential themes and images already appeared in these first versions, it is my impression that they were quite different from the definitive texts as they now stand. Probably the idea of writing a book about New York developed later, and those first poems were only isolated attempts to express the double experience and feelings that his loneliness and the shock of the new reality—'the extra-human architecture,' 'the furious rhythm of geometry and anguish'—produced in him.

These had to be transformed, by a driving inner force, into poetry. But in the beginning the force was not as yet channeled into a complete picture or pattern. It is interesting to note that during the first months he read the poems to everyone with whom he came into contact; when the complete book was presumably taking shape in his mind the readings became rarer and he seldom spoke to others of what he was doing. By then the first *impact* must have become an idea; the unconscious compulsion, conscious effort; and perhaps he did not feel entirely sure of what he was doing. It is likely that the first drafts of most of the poems were written, or at least planned, in New York. But most of them were reworked after his departure from the city. In other words, the book is the product of vivid impressions re-created later by the alchemy of memory. Several poems appeared in literary reviews during the following years; and in 1931 he gave a lecture and read part of the work in Madrid. By that time the book must have reached its final stages; but the first posthumous printing by Losada was not complete, and even a very significant poem, "Crucifixion," was not published until 1950 and appears here for the first time in English.

3.

As the book has finally reached us, it has a clear organization externally, as well as an inner sequence of the moods and impulses of the poet.

It is divided into ten sections which rigorously correspond with five alternative moments of spiritual experience:

I. "Poems of Solitude at Columbia University": Here the poet in his loneliness, lost in a strange world, "among shapes turning serpent" (i.e., obeying blind earthly impulses) and those "seeking crystal" (i.e. seeking light), sees himself as 'murdered by heaven,' as a propitiatory victim of the chaos of life and the world. All the images decry mutilation and silence: "the tree-stump now tuneless," the "crack-brained creatures," "the deafmutes of torpor." In the confusion he cannot find his own face, grown strange with the passing of each day. He longs for the eyes of his infancy, or for old friends now frozen and buried and burned in a world made of lust and dissembled objects. He repudiates all knowledge:—'don't ask me anything,' "question no further." All things "find only their vacancy," and in the uninhabited air there is only the grief of emptiness. He will shout for his lost love in vain.

II. Comprising Sections 2 and 3: "The Negroes" and "Streets and Dreams." Here the equation of pain, spiritual vacuity and primitive passion astir in the mechanical jungle is organized around two meaningful motifs of medieval tradition and religious overtones: Paradise Lost and The Dance of Death. The Negro, snatched from the real jungle but still 'nostalgic of pristine blue' and deprived of "the lore of the trunk and the bypath," becomes the symbol of confused humanity in Pandemonium. He is the victim of civilization, while at the same time he preserves intact, under the dark eclipse of the skin, the impulses and strength of man unmarred by original sin. Blood—always for Lorca the image of vital force and tragedy—flushes furiously without finding an outlet:

> You Harlem! You Harlem! You Harlem!
> No anguish to equal your thwarted vermilions,
> your blood-shaken, darkened eclipses,

or

> Blood has no doors in your night, lying face to the sky.
> Nowhere a blush. But under the skins, blood is raging,
> alive in the spine of a dagger and the breast of a landscape,

and the great king, the new Adam, imprisoned in a janitor's suit, in the clamor of elevators, dusters, graters and casseroles, gives vent to his people's fury with his spoon, gouging out the crocodile's eyes and thumping on the monkey-rumps.

This interpretation does not clarify the accumulative rush of metaphors, allusions and symbols, almost impossible to decipher. It tends only to suggest a meaning. The important thing is that few readers will fail to grasp the impression of sympathy and indignation that the poet tries to convey.

In the following section he presents the picture of the modern city, as he sees it, in a series of poems, "Streets and Dreams," introduced by the dance of death presided over by the grotesque Mask advancing through a desolate urban landscape. Here it is not the dead who come to the dance, but the living. The spirit has vanished. It is the time for the 'parched,' 'the dry things' and the 'definitive silence'—the time for the massive assembly of 'animal death' and ruins.

The light of creation is forgotten, everything becomes shifting: "half a planet was sand, the other half, . . . quicksilver." The world subjugated, enslaved by lust and power, is ready for total destruction:

> Between columns of numbers and blood, the mask cuts its figure
> between tempests of gold and the groans of the jobless
> howling the epoch's extinction of light, in nighttime's obscurity,
> O savage and shameless America! Savage
> supine on your snowy frontiers!

The time for 'cobras' and 'nettle' to climb up to the last levels and to take possession through patios and roof-gardens is approaching; for 'lianas' shall follow the rifles.

After this impressive dance of death which brings to mind the visions of a Patinir, a Brueghel or a Bosch, there are some poems of extreme, almost repellent, realism, such as "Landscape of Vomiting Multitudes (Coney Island Dusk)" and "Landscape of the Urinating Multitudes (Battery Place Nocturne)," alternating with others of a visionary or somnambulistic nature. The climax is reached in "Unsleeping City (Brooklyn Bridge Nocturne)," where the oneiric fantasy is effectively blended with the universal vigil in the face of death, threatening everywhere: "the spawn of the moon [a permanent symbol of death in all Lorca's poetry] sniff the cabins, and circle. The living iguanas arrive and set tooth on the sleepless."

No one can escape and no one should relax from the vigil:

> No sleep in the sky; nobody, nobody.
> No one lies sleeping.

Because grief and death are the inseparable companions of man:

> Whomsoever his woe brings to grief, it will grieve without quarter.
> Whom death brings to dread will carry that death on his shoulders.

Only in unrelenting vigilance may there be a possibility of redemption, for life is no dream but a collective insomnia.

> No one lies sleeping.
> And should one shut an eye,
> lay on the whip, my boys, lay on the whip!

Meanwhile the poet looks at the night in the midst of a sort of cosmic solitude ("a planet alone in a heaven alone") for the signs of a new dawn: "Christmas on the Hudson," "Birth of Christ," "Dawn." The world is not yet ready for the new light: dawn comes, but there is no mouth to receive it, as in a new communion, "for here neither morning nor promise is possible."

Nevertheless, in the darkness of anxiety we perceive a note of hope. "Blind Panorama of New York" ends with an affirmation of the persistence of the world.

> No woe in our voices. Here only our planet persists.
> Our earth, with its gates of forever,
> that give on the flush of its fruits.

III. Sections 4, "Poems from Lake Eden Mills," and 5, "In the Farmer's Cabin," form a sort of bucolic interlude. Chronologically, they do not correspond to the actual experience of the poet, since we know his stay in the country took place in the late part of the summer, prior to the writing of the majority of the poems of "Streets and Dreams," dated around December. But, in the special time of the poetic scheme, they are well placed here. They represent a moment of stillness in the frenzied anxiety characterizing the first reaction of the author in the poems that we have discussed, as if he were finally awakening from a nightmare; an effort to escape towards more serene and luminous spheres. They also represent in the stylistic development of the book a sort of transition between the incoherence of the first poems, more personal in tone, and the impersonal and abstract ones that followed.

In the peace of the countryside the poet regains his emotional equilibrium. The opening poem of Section 4 has an epigraph from Garcilaso, a Spanish pastoral poet of the Renaissance, that is all placidity: "Our herd is grazing, the wind breathes." The poet seeks to regain his voice of old, which did not know "the flow of the thick and the bitter," the voice of candor and love, "voice of my opening side."

Furthermore, he wishes to re-enter the lost Paradise:

> Let me pass by that gate
> where Eve gnaws the ant
> and Adam impregnates a dazzle of fish.

The next poem bears the title "Heaven Alive." Thereafter, in the section called "In the Farmer's Cabin," the becalmed tone persists, but a strange feeling of a new presence of death filters through numerous subdued allusions: "the blind horses," "the door of dark water," "the diminutive fevers," 'the cancer, at midnight in the passage-way,' "the beds where the guests of contagion lay dying."

This subtle presence of death, as if emerging surreptitiously from nowhere, becomes the dominant theme in the following section, which undoubtedly forms the axis of the whole book, "Introduction to Death: Poems of Solitude in Vermont." But now the mood has completely changed. The poet has probably by this time conquered the emotional crisis which made him respond so earnestly to the disquieting signs of confusion. His solitude is now more meditative than emotional; his language becomes clearer, his thought more meaningful. What he sees and expresses is still the triumph of death, of emptiness—although no more in a tragic masquerade but rather as a universal, moving, depersonalized force.

As in the first lines of the first poem, where he saw shapes or forms losing their sense, so now it is not only the forms but the essence of things that is being lost. As in a new chaos, every being strives to be something else. Death, totally dehumanized, is expressed in a general mutation of everything that exists, fleeing its own essence:

> The strain of it!
> Horse would be dog,
> dog would be swallow,
> swallow, a wasp,
> wasp would be horse!
> And the horse—
> ....
> And the rose—
> ....
> And the sugar—
> ....

The poet himself is not free from this sense of transmutation. Once more he appears as a witness of the upheaval:

> And I, on the eaves,
> who strain to be fiery seraph, and am—

A further step and we find ourselves in total emptiness: "Nocturne of the Void:"

> *To see how all passes,*
> *the void and the vesture together,*
> *give me your gauntlet of moonlight,*
> *and that other glove, lost in the grass,*
> *O my love!*
> ....
> See how the shapes of concretion seek out their vacancy.

And further on, in "Ruin," even the most immaterial, incorporeal things disappear into Nothing:

> Still unencountered,
> wayfarer in his own white torso,
> so went the wind.

The recurrent motif of primeval creation is still present. Here and in the following poem, "Moon and Insect Panorama: Love Poem," the moon (death) presides over total dissolution, but grass and insects represent the persistence of life:

> The grasses have come. Child,
> the spittle blades chime
> under hollow heaven.

and

> The insects,
> The insects alone,
> the cracklers, the stingers, the tremblers, the swarmers,
> and the moon
> sunk in the door of its ruins, with a gauntlet of smoke.

IV. In his solitude the poet has seen the course of things clearly. No more doubt or confusion: on returning to the city (Section 7), he will raise an indignant voice to denounce the senseless massacre of a civilization that has destroyed life with its materialism. In "New York: Office and Denunciation" the whole city appears drowned in an inundation of blood: all living things—ducks, hogs, lambs, man—are crushed by economic multiplications and furor.

Nonetheless, redemption shall come. In a new crucifixion, the crucifixion of humanity, blood shall move away, like a bleating of lambs behind the drunkards:

> So it befell, on a time;
> and the whole earth awakened . . .

This poem, "Crucifixion," was not published, as we have already said, until 1950. It has appeared for the first time incorporated at the end of *Poeta en Nueva York* in the recent Spanish edition of the complete works of Lorca. Mr. Belitt has rightly placed it here. Independently of the external reasons that he gives in an appendix, it is evident that it fits perfectly into the pattern of the book where it has been placed.

V. The poet is now ready to leave, in a flight, as he puts it, toward civilization, but not before raising his voice, a scorching clamor of protest, in two Odes—probably the two most powerful poems of the book. He climbs the highest tower so that his shouting may be heard, and in his "Cry to Rome: From the Chrysler Building Tower" he hurls to the winds a potent indictment in which the betrayal of the spirit of Christianity is mixed with a prophetic vision of human slavery and war.

> For see: there is none to apportion the bread and the wine
> or cultivate grass in the mouths of the dead,
> none to turn back the linens of quiet
> or weep for the elephant's wounds.
> Only the blacksmiths,
> a million, to temper the chains for the still-to-be-born.
> Only carpenters,
> a million, to hammer the coffins unmarked by a cross.
> Only a rout of laments.
> undoing their clothing and awaiting the bullet.

Man has forgotten the two sources of life, natural as well as spiritual, 'the mystery of the corn tassel' or "Christ giving water eternally," and the earth is invaded by "sewers," "black nymphs of cholera," and "the serpents of famine." But the persistent myths of Christian redemption and Paradise Regained can never be destroyed. All victims shall cry for the "daily bread," the "flower of the alder" and the "threshed tenderness" until "earth's will be done . . . who offers her harvest to all."

In closing, he turns his voice to Walt Whitman, the great poet of Mannahatta, to decry the corruption of modern man, betrayer of Whitman's democratic faith. Again we see the image of a world in anguish:

> Agony, agony, dream, ferment and dream.
> It is the world's way, my friend: agony, agony.
> Under the town-clock the dead decompose.
> War takes its course with a million gray sewer-rats, sobbing.

While

> The well-to-do will to their darlings
> little candle-lit death-beds,
> and life is not noble, or wholesome, or holy.

Whitman's dream of a healthy love for the pure human being has been corrupted by ignoble perversion, and his prophecy of a powerful America where a new humanity would overcome pain and injustice and would feel strong, like the rivers, has come to naught:

> Sleep on; for nothing abides.
> A dancing of walls rocks the meadows
> and America drowns under engines and tears.

In spite of everything, hope again closes the poem and, for all practical purposes, the book. The poet ends by invoking a strong wind from the deepest abyss of the night to clear the way for a new Dawn, when a Negro child, the incarnation of primeval innocence, shall announce the coming of the 'kingdom of the ears of grain,' eternal symbol of fertility.

The two last sections of the book, "Flight from New York" and "The Poet Arrives in Habana," simply express the end of the voyage, the awakening on gayer shores, where the poet reëncounters his old voice in the realms of the Cuban Negro and returns to his folkloric inspiration of happier times.

4.

An attempt has been made to interpret the structure of the book in its relation to the experience of the poet, by establishing a sort of logical sequence in what otherwise appears to be an arbitrary array of images and, at times, of shocking unpoetic dicta. Our analysis proves, if we are not mistaken, that this apparently nightmarish vision of the city and of modern life has a clear pattern, which results in an organic unity built around strong and powerful motives. It does not matter whether we attribute this unity to an automatic revelation of a deeper reality, as a surrealist may claim, or to a conscious and well-conceived scheme.

But even if our interpretation is right, we realize that this is not all. Every rational analysis of poetry is wanting in what really constitutes true poetic perception, because the poet does not explain reality but reacts to it in his own peculiar language. Poetry conveys feeling, communicates experience, and is below and above rational and historical understanding. It deals with certain truths. Its language is a language of symbols, signals and images, set in rhythm with a special time or tempo, which awake a certain type of response in the reader, shaken or moved into contemplation or awakened to the mystery of things.

This is why true criticism of poetry should deal primarily with poetic structure and language rather than with ideas or even sentiments; should strive to explain how the different elements that the poet uses find their place and order—a peculiar order—in the poem. Such a task, however, is considerably beyond the scope of the present writer's purpose, which is merely that of opening a door to a meaningful reading. At the most we can simply suggest what some of those elements are and what their function is in the work.

As regards style, the outstanding features of the book, perceptible at a single reading without detailed analysis, are richness, confusion, and an interchangeable quality of linguistic symbols carried to extremes. No effort has been made at any statistical computation;

but it is my impression nevertheless that more than in any other of Lorca's works the predominant form here is the substantive. These substantives are seldom abstract nouns, but refer to all existing organic and inorganic beings and matter—animals, minerals, plants, natural phenomena, objects of the mechanical and man-created world—and also to the world of human desires and emotions. Adjectives are seldom descriptive and very rarely those which one would expect to associate with the nouns they modify. The same could be said of the abundance of adverbial phrases and, in general, of almost every word. A great number of verbs are, we believe, verbs of movement conveying ideas of change and destruction with a very dynamic connotation: *go, search, stumble, dissolve, crumble, agitate, bristle*. Every word has a strong sensory, rather than an ideological or emotional, charge, and almost all of them are used in a metaphorical sense within a metaphorical system, based mainly on distant and inconceivable associations: the most unrelated forms are brought together; properties, qualities, and functions attributed to objects are often in total opposition to their nature. Thus, the concrete becomes abstract; the physical is humanized; the emotional becomes inert or mechanical or automatic, and vice versa. Earth, heaven, water, fire, birds transformed into oxen, crystallized fishes, swallows with crutches — everything loses its identity.

In this way the style of the whole book is characterized by an extreme violent *metagoge,* which, together with chaotic enumerations and a constant feeling of hallucination, transmits the idea that the world is in a restless turmoil, ruled by permanent metamorphosis. Most of this has been commonly associated with surrealism; and, indeed, it could be said that Lorca here follows faithfully the conception of art expounded by Lautréamont, which surrealists made their own: "Art is a fortuitous encounter of a sewing machine and an umbrella on a dissecting table."

The difference here is that Lorca's book has nothing capricious about it, nothing ironical, unless we think in terms of a transcendental irony. The poet may have failed in communicating his sense of horror and preoccupation, but there is no doubt that he was talking in earnest when he denounced the disorder of the world as he saw it in this ultra-modern city, representative of the most advanced stage of civilization. He was not the first to cry havoc in behalf of both a continent and the whole panorama of the occidental world, whose doom Spengler prophesied in a book today virtually forgotten but of great influence after the First World War. Other Europeans visiting the 'brave new world' had expressed similar warnings. Duhamel, in *Scènes de la Future*, Huxley and many others had reacted similarly. There was at the time a whole legion of poets of gloom. And in America, from Henry Adams through the new humanism up to Waldo Frank and the then most important novelists from Dreiser to Upton Sinclair, Sinclair Lewis and John Dos Passos, there was a score of writers either depicting the corruption of life or expressing similar uneasiness about the trends of the twentieth century. All this Lorca knew; and it undoubtedly formed the background of an attitude which, as we have said in the beginning, was a result in part of the Depression that he witnessed.

Being a poet, he did not analyze or describe, he *felt*—and his feeling took the form of thematic images. There are a few which appear very soon, in the first poems, and are constantly repeated until they become leitmotifs: 'things without roots,' 'flight and dissolution of forms,' 'forgetfulness of heaven,' 'lack of outlet,' 'struggle,' and especially 'emptiness,' 'vacuity,' 'hollowness,' 'void.'

But perhaps more revealing than these recurrent themes and images, is the fact that all the elements of the book's style are organized in a dynamic and at the same time dialectic tension, as a result of seeing the world of reality torn by a permanent duality and conflict. This takes many forms: natural, religious, or conceptual: birth and death, heaven and earth, sin and redemption, geometry and anguish, spirit and passion, man in his constant clash with matter. All are related to a single all-embracing idea: the return to primitive, destructive instincts and passions let loose by a mechanical civilization, deprived of Grace or, as it were, in rebellion against the spirit. The contrast is one between the primitiveness of human appetites without moral restraints, and

xxviii

the perfection of technology: man, emptied of his spiritual content in a mechanized world, returns to barbarity. The result is a self-destructive confusion, as if the crumbling of this man-created chaos is necessary for the rising of a new life in which nature and the spirit will find harmony. The book is not so much an impression of New York as an indictment of modern civilization.

We have shown that it corresponds to a conception prevalent among many intellectuals of the twenties and thirties, shocked by the traces of suffering and disorder left by the First World War in the form of economic depression and upheaval. But Lorca was no philosopher or historian or sociologist. He was a poet, and it is the poetic quality of the book that still gives it meaning, while many treatises of the same epoch have been forgotten. It is the force of his vision, together with the constant readiness of the poet to testify in behalf of it, that endows these poems with a sort of apocalyptic revelation. What Leon Bloy said of Lautréamont could well be applied here: "The unquestionable sign of every poet is the prophetic unconsciousness, the disturbing faculty of uttering to all men and at all times strange words, whose meaning he himself does not comprehend."

No one can deny today, twenty-five years after these inspired poems were written, that their prophecy became to a certain extent reality; that the omens of war and destruction repeated obsessively or expressed directly more than once, as in "Little Boy Stanton"—"when the tumult of war begins"—were in great part fulfilled and still sound disturbing in an atomic age.

It is this prophetic quality of the book that led Juan Larrea—interpreter of the "Guernica" of Picasso and himself a poet obsessed with the prophetic essence of poetry and the portents that it reveals—to make a striking observation. It was Larrea's belief that in this book Lorca, by yielding his verbal person to the chance of poetic automatism and by abandoning himself to the psychic volcanism where oracles take shape, let the collective unconscious express itself, and thus became the voice of a supra-real and supra-historical force which rules the hidden course of history.

Larrea furthermore sees that the poet himself announced unconsciously his own tragic destiny and sacrifice. It does not matter whether or not we believe in the power of vaticination in poetry. There is undoubtedly something very mysterious and troubling, in view of the violent end of the poet and the failure of all efforts to ascertain the place of his burial, in his obsession with blood in the very first line in which he presents himself as "murdered by heaven," or in passages such as the following, in the third poem quoted by Larrea:

> When the pure forms collapsed
> in the *cri-cri* of daisies,
> it came to me how they had murdered me too.
> They ransacked the cafés, the graveyards, the churches,
> they opened the wine-casks and clothes-presses,
> they ravaged three skeletons to gouge out the gold of their teeth.
> But me, they never encountered.
> They never encountered me?
> No. Never encountered me.

5.

In any complete study of the book, besides a careful stylistic analysis, three questions should be clarified by critics of the future: its relationship to American literature and, in a minor degree, to foreign literature bearing on the subject; its relationship to the Negro theme; and, mainly, its relationship to surrealism. Without attempting to give a complete answer to any of them, I shall try to submit some exploratory remarks.

In regard to the first, it can be safely affirmed that the poet knew little, at least directly, of modern American literature. Lorca had a remarkable impatience with any language other than Spanish. Practically all he read of foreign literature he read in translation. There were few books in his room in John Jay, and he was busy not only absorbing the impressions of the city but also in writing a great deal of his own verse, as we have pointed out. Of the books that he read while in New York there are two which may have some significance as indirect sources: *Manhattan Transfer* by Dos Passos and *All Quiet on the Western Front* by Eric Remarque, both in Spanish translations. A more direct connection could be established with *The Waste Land* of Eliot which undoubtedly he read in the Spanish translation, *Tierra baldía,* of Angel Flores.

It is very difficult to conceive of two more different poets than Eliot and Lorca—the first a thoroughly cerebral poet, the second an astonishing example of what we may call the natural poet. The two works, *The Waste Land* and *Poet in New York,* are also entirely different. Nevertheless, a comparison between the two could be very fruitful. There is not only a similarity in mood and in the main theme of death, destruction and the end in nothingness of modern civilization, but also, what is more important, a striking coincidence in vocabulary and imagery. Even the phrase construction and the rhythm of many lines in the Flores translation remind us very frequently of *Poet in New York,* and here and there an almost exact verbal analogy can be found, as when Lorca says in "New York: Office and Denunciation":

> What shall I do now? Align all the landscapes?

which immediately brings to mind two lines—widely separated, it is true—of *The Waste Land*:

> What shall I do now? What shall I do now?
> ....
> Shall I at least set my lands in order?

A more difficult task would be to establish concretely Lorca's debt to Whitman. That he understood Whitman and had a clear idea of his message is evident in his Ode. The numerous repetitions, the chaotic enumerations, the length of the lines, the prophetic tone, the constant use of the first person, the great imaginative fluency and the cosmic breadth show without doubt that he had absorbed also a good deal of Whitman's style and mannerisms.

Nevertheless, it could be misleading to measure the extent of his knowledge of Whitman's work without a closer analysis. In general, the matter of influence in Lorca is an extremely complicated one. Sometimes he pretended to know less than he really knew, perhaps to differentiate himself as a "born" poet from other poets of his generation who were of strong intellectual temper. He had, furthermore, an extraordinary facility for assimilating for his own purposes whatever literary or artistic current was at the moment in the air; a few allusions, some conversations or some cursory reading sufficed. It was almost like a sixth sense, like a physical attribute.

Our guess regarding Whitman would be that most of the Whitmanisms of the book came through Lorca's friendship here in New York with León Felipe (one of the most important Spanish translators of the Camden poet), who, during the year he knew Lorca, was immersed in Whitman's social and democratic faith. There is also, as in the case of Eliot, a great distance between the sensibility and creative power of Lorca and the moral and social inspiration of León Felipe. But there is no doubt in my mind that at least in the point of departure Lorca's conversations with the Spanish author of *Versos y oraciones de caminante* left some important trace in his attitude towards his subject and induced him to read Whitman, of whose work there were several Spanish translations.

In connection with the Negro theme, it should be remembered that it was very much in vogue at the time as a result of the neo-primitivism in art and poetry and of the literary Africanism of writers like Vachel Lindsay and Paul Morand. Lorca was also naturally drawn to it by the same temperamental reasons which made him the singer of gypsies: his feeling, as a poet and a dramatist, for primitive, earthy passions; his feeling, as an artist, for rhythm and traditional music as well as movement, gesture, and color. Negro literature and poetry, either by Negro authors or as a theme for others, had at the moment great success and was beginning to shape into an important movement in some Spanish-speaking countries, especially Cuba and Puerto Rico. Federico knew this and felt the attraction not only of the theme in itself but also of the melody, rhythm, and dramatic texture of Negro spirituals, many of which he learned by heart to increase his rich collection of folkloric songs. In spite of this, it is very doubtful that he knew at the time, directly, much of the new Negro-inspired literature. His Negro motifs, so powerful in the book as to constitute one of the dominant themes, came, as did most of the other motifs, from direct impression and contact. The King of Harlem was born entirely in the poet's imagination.

More important for an understanding of the work is the need to clarify its connection with surrealist art. Lorca was at the time inclined towards surrealism and it could be said that this is the first important work that the movement produced in Spain. This is an aspect of Lorca's evolution that nobody has yet studied. When someone does, several things should be borne in mind.

The earliest contact with surrealism in Spain was probably a lecture given by Louis Aragon on April 18, 1925 at the Residencia de Estudiantes at Madrid, where he lived; it was partially published later with the title "Fragments d'une conférence" in the magazine *La Révolution Surréaliste* (no. 4, 15 juillet 1925). Although it probably caused some scandal among the very small group of vanguard writers in Madrid, it seems to have been soon forgotten. We have not found any allusion to it in the Spanish press. Few of those connected with the development of the movement in Spanish letters remember it, and the only record we have come across is found in the *Histoire du Surréalisme* (Paris: Editions de Seuil, 1945) of Maurice Nadeau.

To judge by the fragments published, it was an invective against bankers, students, bureaucrats—against work and science: "Je maudis la science, cette soeur jumelle du travail." Aragon condemned civilization in general and said, among other things:

Êtes-vous jamais descendus au fond de ce puits noir? Qu'y avez-vous trouvé, quelle galeries vers le ciel? ... Nous aurons raison de tout. Et d'abord nous ruinerons cette civilisation qui vous est chère, où vous êtes moulés comme des fossiles dans le schiste. L'ère de metamorphose est ouverte. ... Je ferai jaillir le sang blond des pavés. ... Monde occidental, tu es condamné à mort. ... Nous réveillerons partout les germes de la confusion et du malaise. Nous sommes les agitateurs de l'esprit. Toutes les barricades sont bonnes, toutes les entraves à vos bonheurs maudits. Juifs, sortez des ghettos. Qu'on affame le peuple, afin qu'il connaisse enfin le goût du pain de colère. ... Et que les trafiquants de drogue se jettent sur nos pays terrifiés. Que l'Amerique au loin croule de ses buildings blancs au milieu des prohibitions absurdes. Soulève-toi, monde! Voyez comme cette terre est sèche et bonne pour tous les incendies. On dirait de la paille.

It is by no means certain that Lorca heard this lecture. Surprisingly, though, we find a clear echo of some of Aragon's remarks in Lorca's poems five years later. The similarities are not only in mood and ideas but also in idiom: 'the era of metamorphosis,' 'the seeds of confusion and distress,' 'the black wells,' 'the dope-peddlers,' 'the bread of wrath,' 'the crumbling of white buildings,' 'the blond blood of pavements.'

By 1927 or 1928, two years after the Aragon lecture, there was much talk of surrealism among some artistic minorities in Madrid. Poets like Juan Larrea and, especially, Alberti, the latter a friendly rival of Lorca, had made the first attempts at surrealist poetry. It was, furthermore, the period of the close friendship—almost artistic partnership—between Lorca and Salvador Dali, leaders of a group which counted, among others, Luis Buñuel, who later became one of the main exponents of surrealist movies. In 1929—the same year that Lorca came to New York—Dali went to Paris to create something like a revolution in surrealist art by practicing his theory of the "irrational object," which was to take the place of the narration of dreams and automatic writing. Roy Campbell, in some strikingly inept remarks, has placed at the door of Dali the main responsibility for what he conceives to be the negative aspects of *Poet in New York*:

Lorca went and stayed in the U.S.A. for some time, but was unable to establish a real contact with the Americans or their way of life. The result on his poetry was entirely negative. He underwent while there the intellectual influence, if not domination, of Salvador Dali, his friend, who is also a great artist of international repute, but a far more complicated personality than Lorca, more resilient and aggressive, with a far wider range of sympathies and interests, and at home anywhere from the U.S.A. to Catalonia. Lorca attempted to follow the Catalonian into the complex world of surrealism, and lost his depth. In Lorca's New York poems, the *Poeta en Nueva York*, his metaphors and images fall out of focus; his verse becomes loose, plaintive, and slightly mephitic.

Apart from the facts that the visits of Dali and Lorca to New York did not coincide (Dali arrived for the first time more than one year later), and that their friendship had by that time considerably cooled, it would be an interesting endeavor to study who influenced whom during the days of close friendship between the two artists. Granted that Lorca was easily, although superficially and fleetingly influenced by friends and new esthetic creeds; granted that Dali had probably a greater grasp of and facility for theoretical ingenuity; granted also that the similarity in imagery between some of Lorca's poems and Dali's paintings of that time is such that no better illustrator could have been found for *Poet in New York* than the Catalonian creator of the "surrealist object"; nonetheless, Lorca was by far the superior in poetic inventiveness and depth. It might be added that during the days in New York Lorca spoke often of Lautréamont (whose *Chants de Maldoror* Dali was going to illustrate) and of Blake, both acclaimed as masters by the surrealists. In spite of all similarities, the book was born of a very personal, perhaps semiconscious, experience. Whatever connections with surrealism can be found, Lorca's vision springs from roots that have little in common with the intellectual or theoretical tenets of official surrealism.

When Lorca writes in "Double Poem of Lake Eden":

> Am neither all poet, all man, or all leaf,
> but only the pulse of a wound that probes to the opposite side.

or later in "New York: Office and Denunciation":

> . . . But I have not come here to ogle the sky.
> Am here to look upon blood, the silt
> in the blood that delivers the engines over the waterfalls
> and our souls to the fang of the cobra.

he is giving expression to a collective and at the same time very real sorrow far removed from the absolute and cold impersonality of most surrealist art and literature. There is also, as we have shown, a strange correspondence between external reality and the innermost thought and feeling of the poet.

There is no doubt that in form, content, and attitude a coincidence with surrealism exists; but Conrad Aiken was entirely right when he said that to call Lorca a surrealist was a mistake: "For to be a surrealist," he explains, "is to be something else than a poet: surrealism is perhaps one of many names, merely, for the substratum out of which poetry is made." And he adds with great insight: "Lorca devoured all the properties of surrealism, stuffed his cheek with them, like a conjurer, blew them out of his mouth again as poems—but so he did with everything else that he fed on."

Keeping this in mind, one should not forget that this book is above all lyrical poetry of high order—poetry made, perhaps, of a different stuff from that most commonly found in the rest of Lorca's work. It can be said that the poet fails at times in communicating his message and that he is frequently lost in an imagistic labyrinth. But on the whole the book is absolutely authentic. As in the rest of almost all Lorca's poetry and drama, the main source here is vivid experience, and the fundamental creative elements are based on direct impressions which in many instances could easily be localized. They are concrete sensations subjected later to an imaginative process which turns them unreal.

This process, analyzed in my previous study of the poet, may be considered briefly in connection with a study of the genesis of some of the New York poems, especially "Little Girl Drowned in the Well," to illustrate Lorca's methods. It is among the most characteristically surrealistic poems in the book. Everything in it seems to be the product of a hallucination; nevertheless, most of its images proceed from immediate sensations perceived in a definite place. Lorca himself explained its origin in a somewhat apocryphal version recorded by the Argentine poet José González Carvalho. He told how at the farm where he was staying,

he had two little friends, a boy and a girl, for whom he would invent legends and improvise songs. In the farmhouse where the children lived . . . there was also a man who was gravely ill, and a blind horse that drew water from the draw well. For Federico, the blind horse had the significance of horror. One day the little girl was found drowned in the well, and Lorca gloomily abandoned the place; later he wrote the magnificent, dark lines in her memory.

What is true in this fabrication is the description of place, as well as the existence of the two children and the illness of the farmer their parent. The *death* of the little girl and the "fact" that he gloomily abandoned the place thereafter are a product of Lorca's inventive fancy, undoubtedly added to give dramatic color to the narrative or perhaps to throw off the track, as artists often do, those who seek logical explanations of artistic creation. It is important to correct the point about the dead child; for giving the poem a motivation that is anecdotical, realistic, and personal deprives it of its significance as poetic creation.

We can add, on the other hand, some topographical details which are very significant for an understanding of the mechanism of

Lorca's imagination. We were with the poet during the days he spent in the Catskills; he read us the poem soon after it had been written, and we are consequently precisely aware of the elements that the poet took as a point of departure. Near the farm, where everything seemed abandoned, there were several great pits that had once been quarries. The place, with its bleeding earth and skeletal rocks, had a desolate grandeur. It was, Federico used to say, like a lunar landscape. The water in the pits could not be seen; but one could hear its murmuring crash at the bottom.

The inspiration for the poem was not born from the inexact anecdote of the dead child but precisely from the contrast between the spontaneous gaiety of the farmer's children and the sadness of the atmosphere. The several elements which enter into the imagery of the poem correspond to concrete things: the coffins (suggested by the sickness of the owner), 'the shores of a horse's eye,' 'the croak [like the frogs of the night] of the tender stars,' and, above all, 'the combat of roots and foreseen solitude' and "the water that never disgorges," which give the whole poem its sense of fascinating unreality and reflect the impression produced on Lorca by the place.

Similarly, it was the atmosphere of Shandaken, in the Catskills, that inspired "Landscape with Two Graves and an Assyrian Dog." On the farm was an enormous dog, old and half blind, which frequently slept in the corridor outside the door of Lorca's room. The terror this produced in him and his obsession with the disease of the farmer—a cancerous sore—appear unconsciously transformed into oneiric images.

> Friend,
> rouse yourself, listen!
> the Assyrian dog howls.
> Cancer's three nymphs have been dancing,
> my son.

In the same way the real background of the imagery in many poems can be localized. What is significant in all this is that it helps us to understand the sensory character of Lorca's poetic creation, so different in this respect from other contemporary poets, in whom poetry is either born of a definite idea or sentiment or, in the case of the surrealists, of a willed and self-conscious unconsciousness. But in our author poetry explodes almost like a force which superimposes upon the conscious artistry the spontaneous vibrations of his temperament, whose fundamental notes are most frequently translated into dramatic substance and imaginative tension, acquiring at the same time a sort of natural cosmic breadth. Clear ideas, logical expression, were not Lorca's realm, which was rather a sort of magic inspiration or magic realism with significant glimpses of the ultimate mystery of things expressed through subconscious intuitions.

In a certain sense it could be said that Lorca was more surrealist than the surrealists. The difference, among others already shown, is that Lorca never could have accepted the materialistic creed and pure rational irrationality of official surrealism. He was a believer in the spirit and in human emotions, with deep, perhaps submerged, religious preoccupations. That fact and a sort of superconsciousness, rather than subconsciousness, explain the surprising organic unity of the book—in fact, of all Lorca's work—in spite of its apparent incoherence.

This superconsciousness, as well as the main attitudes visible in *Poet in New York,* is clarified if we relate the book to two previous poems, written before his trip, in which we find the same strong desire to find an order in the confusion of the modern world: his "Ode to Salvador Dali" and especially his "Ode to the Most Blessed Sacrament." Here also Lorca strives to make us feel the anguish of the modern world, the pain of life assaulted by the desires of the flesh, the horror of blood and of sin, the darkness of human passions. And here also the contemplation of the dismal fate without hope is converted into yearning for peace and love and order:

> Thy Sacrament of light in equilibrium only,
> could quiet the anguish of love that knew no bound,
> O World, now have you an end for your forsakenness
> for your perennial horror of bottomless pit
> O captive Lamb of the three consistent voices!
> Immutable Sacrament of discipline and love!

In my opinion it is in its twofold character as a testimony of a disrupted reality revealed directly in poetic symbols, and as a vision of a higher spiritual order—as well as in its consummate richness of imagination—that this book has its meaning today and that its enduring value as a poetic document of a troubled epoch is assured.

This also justifies Mr. Belitt's attempt to give, through his translation, a clearer meaning for English-speaking readers than the work had in previous renderings. Those who know the Spanish text will immediately see that Mr. Belitt has taken, at times, liberties which might seem excessive. Others, misled by the obscurity of the text, might blame the translator for the incoherence that is in the original. Mr. Belitt's intent has been, we believe, not so much to give a literal translation as to re-create the original in terms of poetry. For this purpose, the two main liberties he has taken are the occasional transposition of terms in the metaphor when it was required either by the rhythm of the line or the character of the language, and the free interpretation of images or concepts which are far from clear in the original. When the complexity of the task is taken into consideration, it will be difficult to deny that most of the time Mr. Belitt has succeeded in transposing to poetic English terms not only the language but also a great deal of the substance and mood of the poems. His is a great service to the understanding of Lorca and also to modern poetry, in which we think that this book has a definite place.

ÁNGEL DEL RÍO.

New York 1955

TRANSLATOR'S FOREWORD

No apology, I hope, is needed for the new translation of a work which refers its author most directly to the American reader. It was to American readers in the broadest sense of the term—the readers of Neruda's *Canto general de Chile* and Martinez' *Los senderos ocultos,* as well as to the "vomiting multitudes" of Coney Island and the somnambulists of Brooklyn Bridge—that the poem was initially addressed by its publishers in Mexico, Argentina, and New York, a decade after its completion in Havana and four years after the inexpiable murder of the poet. Today, *Poet in New York* remains an indispensable book for readers of two Americas.

This translator, along with a generation of American readers, is initially in debt to the example of Rolfe Humphries' pioneering version of *Poet in New York,* and to the passion that held him to his task at a time when no fair or definitive text could be found by his publishers in this country. The claim of translators today must be a modest one, by comparison: that of augmenting a provisional and defective text with a full and authoritative one, emending deviant or faulty readings, repairing omissions of punctuation and errors of typography, and limiting the hazards of a poem already famous for its "obscurity" to those which are irreducibly a part of the poet's intention.

To these objectives, I have added another which may furnish the true occasion for the present translation. My concern, in a very real sense, has been a double one: that of exploring a *dimension* of translation, as well as an artifact of contemporary Spanish culture. No translator can long expose himself to the harassing fire of two linguistic happenings—that which is given to him by a poem originally conceived within the contexts of a language not his own, as a completed action; and that which he seeks to create for it out of the resources of his own tongue—and remain incurious of his function.

It has not been my assumption, as it was Mr. Humphries', that these poems "cannot, and should not, be expected to sound . . . like English poems, or American ones." That the "effects of Spanish verse are not ours," and that the English equivalences can never be identical with the Spanish, is both a truism inherent in the modality of language and an enigma inexhaustible to thought. The day when "the whole earth was of one language" is not yet returned, and the generations of Babel continue to plague the translator. His premise, at the outset, must be a hard one: that the *poem* in English will not follow gratuitously upon the poem in Spanish, once the English *word* has followed "accurately" upon the Spanish; that their textures and durations will differ, word by word, and word after word, and that the differences will deepen and compound with unimaginable complexity with the collocations of words; that syntax distributes and assembles identical notions with differing tensions in differing languages; that words, in whatever language, have a history which is not Esperanto or Sanskrit, or the "history of mankind," but the cultural consequence of their activity in the linguistic experience of a group—for chauvinism is an inalienable property of all language; that words must be shouted into, like wells, rather than joined in a series like pipe-lengths; and finally, that for the poet, the momentum of words is as important and mysterious a trust as their matter, and that their momentum—their *brio,* their capacity to reveal the spirit at work within the letter—is rooted irrationally in the densities and ambiguities of the individual language.

Nonetheless, it would be my conviction that a translator who is content with *translating out of* one language only, has completed only one half the transaction, and that the harder task of *translating into* his own remains to be confronted. It is a task, needless to say, full of risk and uncertainty—in the lonely sign of translation where the translator, forever on the *other* side of his original, reconceives the solitude of the creator on *his* side of the binder's seam, and, like the imagining man of Coleridge, "dissolves, dissipates, diffuses," in order to create anew. It is here that the true "morality" of translation may be said to reside, its real conscience: in an exploration of real temptations, real perils, real equivalences, from which the trot and the hack and the self-serving complacencies of the "accurate" way are excluded. Here, in short, the translator is at liberty to contemplate the universe of the given poem as its creator originally contemplated the universe of his given experience —not as a datum substantively present in the nature of things, but as a precarious search for exactitudes, correspondences, analogies which will mirror their model only in flashes, and which will demonstrate nothing so much as its partial knowability in the end.

I should like to acknowledge my gratitude to those who have helped bring this translation to completion and minimize its shortcomings. I am in debt to José F. Montesinos for reading together with me in the Spanish each of the essays and certain of the poems included in this volume; for his illumination of ambiguities and nuances insoluble to myself; for the providential correction of error, and direct insights into the mind and sensibility of the poet which have at times made conjecture seem like a species of inspiration. To Dr. Montesinos—and equally to Dr. Ángel del Río of Columbia University—I owe the additional kindness of a close review of the final manuscript—doubtless less punishing than should be—which has often helped me temper the afflatus of the English to a reading more in keeping with the original, and reconsider the alternatives available to me. I am grateful to the poet's brother, Francisco García Lorca, for his assistance in fixing the Spanish text—which in the main accords with the model of the 1940 Mexican edition—and for additional help in construing images and allusions whose contexts steadfastly eluded me. It would be a disservice to these and other benefactions to imply that the present version fairly reflects the authority of either their intimate acquaintance with the poet or their deeper comprehension of the tradition of Spanish poetry. Nevertheless, I have sought, in all conscience, to measure my choices in the light of their considered responses, and to employ the added resonance as a clue to the fidelity or impertinence of my own efforts.

I have incurred a number of "minor" obligations, each bearing on an impasse which seemed at the time major, which I now have the opportunity to acknowledge. I am obliged to my colleague, Mrs. Nora Montesinos, for entering into a—for her—tedious round of correspondence with friends and family of the poet in my behalf and alleviating by many acts of kindness the vexations of translation; to the poet's sister, presently residing in Madrid, for confirming details relative to uncollected or "missing" poems of *Poet in New York* and transcribing for me, in advance of publication, the canon of the poem from the collected works published by Editorial Aguilar in Spain; to Juan Guerrero, friend and contemporary of the poet, for making available to me a unique text of *"Amantes asesinados por una perdiz"* ("Lovers Slain By A Partridge") and accounting for the circumstances of its "disappearance"; to Donald Allen, for proposing the present translation and imagining me to be capable of it. The Introduction by Ángel del Río, as readers of his admirable study of the poet [1] are already aware, is an exceptional dispensation for audiences in this country and constitutes a literary event in its own right. It leaves the poem in the keeping of a friend uniquely qualified to speak for its original mutations and for a poet who would surely have valued his introduction beyond that of any of his countrymen in the New World.

A word with regard to the Critical Chronology and the Appendices of essays, poems, and fugitive prose pieces which complete the design of this volume. The Chronology, I am bound to confess, is a counsel of desperation arising from the need to encompass a complex and extenuated textual history whose recital in any other form would have numbed the reader. It is my hope that the facts, in their present guise, combine the *longueurs* of bibliography with the spice of amateur detection, and deliver intact the story of a manuscript's total emergence. The aims of the Appendices are several: principally, to impound "missing" or conjectural poems

[1] Ángel del Río, *Federico García Lorca. . . . Vida y obra. etc.* (New York: Hispanic Institute in the United States, 1941). Reprinted as *Vida y obra de Federico García Lorca* ("Estudios Literarios," III [Zaragoza: Heraldo de Aragón, S. A., 1952]).

which fall into the orbit of *Poet in New York,* but whose order in the canon cannot be established for reasons made known in the Chronology; to document the Chronology by every means available to the translator and inaccessible to the general reader; and to suggest the development of Lorca's "surrealist" manner from his earliest exercises in "style" to the visceral agonies of his vision of the City.

Two essays, little known in this country, have also been included in the Appendices, in the belief that *Poet in New York* raises esthetic and compositional problems as dismaying to readers of Lorca's popular *romances* as his tormented use of the New York scene; and that, for such readers, these essays, between jest and earnest, will measure the sources of the poet's imaginative commitment. The essay on Góngora, which William Carlos Williams has commended to all practitioners of poetry "to read and have to heart," is reproduced in a slightly abbreviated version; the essay on the *Duende,* with the exception of certain opening amenities, is translated in full for the first time.

The rewards of these essays, as the reader will readily discover, are considerable, and would require a Foreword beyond the scope of these pages to suggest. Particularly significant, however, is the ambivalence of Lorca's case for both the willed and the mantic in art—for the "inspired state" from which "one returns as from a foreign country," and for the ritual exercise of techniques applied by the poet to their last refinement of intended effectiveness. The "surrealism" of *Poet in New York* involves, obviously, a suspension of those controls: a journey into the adventitious and the nocturnal like that of his Hunter in the forest of the "thousand splendors and the thousand hideous masks of the splendid," or the baroque improvisations of the Girl With the Combs. It culminates in a literature of the *grito*: the *cry,* which has little in common with the Gallic importations of Rafael Alberti or his models in Apollinaire and Breton. Its sources, as his remarkable entertainment on the *Duende* will make clear, are no less regional and Hispanic than the ballads of Lorca's popular manner. Unlike those ballads, however, *Poet in New York* probes *behind* the flamenco invention—behind the impacted spontaneities of the *saeta, siguiriya, petenera, soleá*—to the frenzy, the shudder, the paroxysm, the "deep song" and the "dark root of the cry" out of which they emerge. It moves directly into the savagery of the psychic occasion, to enact an agon of self-knowledge, unmediated by form, in an imagery of blood, spittle, excrement, alcohol, nausea, madness, and cathartic dance.

For if the Gypsy ballads are a tribal and formalized manifestation of the *gitanismo* of García Lorca, the *Poet in New York* is a private improvisation on its sensibility. With good reason Alfredo de la Guardia, in the course of his appraisal of the poem, pauses to ask with unfeigned incredulity:

> *"Ay, Harlem!*
> *Ay, Wall Street!"*

What is the meaning of that *Ay!*—the mark of flamenco lament, the wail of the "deep song"—in a Stock Exchange world that, in the course of that very year (1929), was to scatter the dynamite charge of its stocks and certificates to all sides and explode in a prodigious crash?

For somewhere between the parable of the Hunter, and the "black sounds" (*"sonidos negros"*) of Pastora Pavon, lie the landscapes of Lorca's New York, in the keeping of that daemon who "smashes the styles" and paints with its "fists and its knees in bituminous blacks," and announces "the unending baptism of all newly-created things."

BEN BELITT

1953: Mexico — 1955: Bennington College, Bennington, Vermont

ACKNOWLEDGMENTS

Thanks are due the editors of the following publications for permission to reprint the following translations: "Unsleeping City" and "Double Poem of Lake Eden" from the Summer 1954 issue of *Virginia Quarterly Review*; "Ode to Walt Whitman" from the January 1955 issue of *Poetry* (Chicago); "Crucifixion" from the Winter 1955 issue of *Partisan Review*; and "Your Childhood in Menton" from *Modern Writing No. 2* (Avon), 1954; "Ruin" and a modified version of the essay on "The Poetic Image in Don Luis de Gongora" from Vol. VI, No. 1, 1950 issue of *The Quarterly Review of Literature*. Angel del Río's *Introduction* first appeared in *New World Writing*, 1955.

— B. B.

POET IN NEW YORK

A BÉBÉ Y CARLOS MORLA

Los poemas de este libro están escritos
en la ciudad de Nueva York el año 1929-1930,
en que el poeta vivió como estudiante en
Columbia University.

F.G.L.

This translation is for
MARTHA HILL DAVIES.

B.B.

I POEMAS DE LA SOLEDAD EN COLUMBIA UNIVERSITY

*Furia color de amor
amor color de olvido.*
—Luis Cernuda

VUELTA DE PASEO

Asesinado por el cielo,
entre las formas que van hacia la sierpe
y las formas que buscan el cristal,
dejaré crecer mis cabellos.

Con el árbol de muñones que no canta
y el niño con el blanco rostro de huevo.

Con los animalitos de cabeza rota
y el agua harapienta de los pies secos.

Con todo lo que tiene cansancio sordomudo
y mariposa ahogada en el tintero.

Tropezando con mi rostro distinto de cada día
¡Asesinado por el cielo!

POEMS OF SOLITUDE AT
COLUMBIA UNIVERSITY

> *Rage the color of love*
> *Love, oblivion's color*
> —LUIS CERNUDA

BACK FROM A WALK

Heaven-murdered one,
among shapes turning serpent
and shapes seeking crystal,
I'll let my hair grow long.

With the tree-stump now tuneless
and the egg-white face of a child

With all crack-brained creatures
and the tatter of dry-footed water

With the deafmutes of torpor,
and the butterfly drowned in the inkwell

Shambling each day with my different face
Ah, heaven-murdered one!

1910

Aquellos ojos míos de mil novecientos diez
no vieron enterrar a los muertos,
ni la feria de ceniza del que llora por la madrugada,
ni el corazón que tiembla arrinconado como un caballito de mar.

Aquellos ojos míos de mil novecientos diez
vieron la blanca pared donde orinaban las niñas,
el hocico del toro, la seta venenosa
y una luna incomprensible que iluminaba por los rincones
los pedazos de limón seco bajo el negro duro de las botellas.

Aquellos ojos míos en el cuello de la jaca,
en el seno traspasado de Santa Rosa dormida,
en los tejados del amor, con gemidos y frescas manos,
en un jardín donde los gatos se comían a las ranas.

Desván donde el polvo viejo congrega estatuas y musgos,
cajas que guardan silencio de cangrejos devorados
en el sitio donde el sueño tropezaba con su realidad.
Allí mis pequeños ojos.

No preguntarme nada. He visto que las cosas
cuando buscan su curso encuentran su vacío.
Hay un dolor de huecos por el aire sin gente
y en mis ojos criaturas vestidas ¡sin desnudo!

Nueva York, agosto 1929

1910

(INTERLUDE)

Those eyes of Nineteen-Ten, my very eyes,
saw no dead man buried,
no ashen bazaars of dawn's mourners
nor the heart, in its recess, like sea-horses, wavering.

Those eyes of Nineteen-Ten, my very eyes,
saw only the blank wall, and the girls making water
the bull's snout, the poisonous mushroom
the unthinkable moon that lightened in corners
dry lemon-rinds, by an adamant blackness of bottles.

Those very eyes, held by a pony's neck
or the breast of the pierced Santa Rosa, asleep,
the rooftops of love, love's unabashed fingers and whimpers,
or cats in a garden sating their hunger on frogs.

Attic of statues and mosses, the old dust's assemblage,
chests keeping a shell-plundered stillness of crabs
in the place where the dreamed falters into the actual:
Little eyes, my very eyes: there.

Question no further. All things, I have seen,
that hold to their course find only their vacancy.
The pit's melancholia, uninhabited ether, is there,
and the clothed ones, bereft of their nakedness, under my eyes!

New York, August 1929

FÁBULA Y RUEDA DE LOS TRES AMIGOS

Enrique,
Emilio,
Lorenzo,

Estaban los tres helados:
Enrique por el mundo de las camas;
Emilio por el mundo de los ojos y las heridas de las manos,
Lorenzo por el mundo de las universidades sin tejados.

Lorenzo,
Emilio,
Enrique,

Estaban los tres quemados:
Lorenzo por el mundo de las hojas y las bolas de billar;
Emilio por el mundo de la sangre y los alfileres blancos,
Enrique por el mundo de los muertos y los periódicos abandonados.

Lorenzo,

Emilio,
Enrique,
Estaban los tres enterrados:
Lorenzo en un seno de Flora;
Emilio en la yerta ginebra que se olvida en el vaso,
Enrique en la hormiga, en el mar y en los ojos vacíos de los pájaros.

Lorenzo,

Emilio,
Enrique,
Fueron los tres en mis manos
tres montañas chinas,
tres sombras de caballo,
tres paisajes de nieve y una cabaña de azucenas
por los palomares donde la luna se pone plana bajo el gallo.

Uno

FABLE AND ROUND OF THE THREE FRIENDS

Enrique,
Emilio,
Lorenzo,

Frozen, the three of them:
Enrique in the world of the bed;
Emilio in the world of the eye and the hand's laceration,
Lorenzo in the world of the topless academies.

Lorenzo,
Emilio,
Enrique,

Burning, the three of them:
Lorenzo in the world of the leaves and the cue-balls,
Emilio in the world of white pinpoints and blood,
Enrique in the world of the dead and the castaway tabloids.

Lorenzo,

Emilio,
Enrique,
Buried, the three of them:
Lorenzo in a nipple of Flora;
Emilio in a staling jigger of gin, in the tumbler, forgotten,
Enrique, in the ant, in the sea, in the vacant eyes of the birds.

Lorenzo,

Emilio,
Enrique,
Held in my hands, the three of them,
three Chinese mountains,
three horses' shadows,
three snowy perspectives and a cabin of lilies
among dovecotes where the moon lay outstretched for the
    gamecock.

One

y uno
y uno,
Estaban los tres momificados,
con las moscas del invierno,
con los tinteros que orina el perro y desprecia el vilano,
con la brisa que hiela el corazón de todas las madres,
por los blancos derribos de Júpiter donde meriendan muerte los
	borrachos.

Tres

y dos
y uno,
Los vi perderse llorando y cantando
por un huevo de gallina,
por la noche que enseñaba su esqueleto de tabaco,
por mi dolor lleno de rostros y punzantes esquirlas de luna,
por mi alegría de ruedas dentadas y látigos,
por mi pecho turbado por las palomas,
por mi muerte desierta con un solo paseante equivocado.

Yo había matado la quinta luna
y bebían agua por las fuentes los abanicos y los aplausos.
Tibia leche encerrada de las recién paridas
agitaba las rosas con un largo dolor blanco,
Enrique,

Emilio,
Lorenzo.
Diana es dura,
pero a veces tiene los pechos nublados.
Puede la piedra blanca latir en la sangre del ciervo
y el ciervo puede soñar por los ojos de un caballo.

Cuando se hundieron las formas puras
bajo el cri cri de las margaritas,

and then one
and then one—
Mummied, the three of them,
with the houseflies of winter,
dog's urine in inkwells scorned by the cockle-burr,
with the wind that brings chill to the hearts of the mothers,
in the white demolitions of Jupiter where the drunkards nibble on
      death.

Three

and then two
and then one,
I saw them destroy themselves, sobbing and singing,
for a hen's egg,
for a night that displayed its tobacco-leaf skeleton,
for my woe full of faces and a barb of bone-splintered moon,
for my pleasure in cogwheels and whiplash
for my breast shaken with doves,
for my derelict dying, with a single mistaken bypasser.

    I had killed the fifth moon
and the fans and the handclapping drank at the fountains.
The milk of the newly-delivered, still tepid and sealed,
troubled the roses with its great white grief.
Enrique,

Emilio,
Lorenzo.
Diana is hard,
but sometimes her bosom goes cloudy.
Even the white stone may pulse in the blood of a stag
and the stag have its dream in the eyes of a stallion.

    When the pure forms collapsed
in the *cri-cri* of daisies,

9

comprendí que me habían asesinado.
Recorrieron los cafés y los cementerios y las iglesias,
abrieron los toneles y los armarios,
destrozaron tres esqueletos para arrancar sus dientes de oro.
Ya no me encontraron.
¿No me encontraron?
No. No me encontraron.
Pero se supo que la sexta luna huyó torrente arriba,
y que el mar recordó ¡de pronto!
los nombres de todos sus ahogados.

it came to me how they had murdered me too.
They ransacked the cafés, the graveyards, the churches,
they opened the wine-casks and clothes-presses,
they ravaged three skeletons to gouge out the gold of their teeth.
But me, they never encountered.
They never encountered me?
No. Never encountered me.
Still, it was known that the sixth moon fled up the torrent,
and the sea could remember—so suddenly!—
the rout of its drowners by name.

TU INFANCIA EN MENTON

Sí, tu niñez, ya fábula de fuentes.

—JORGE GUILLÉN

Sí, tu niñez ya fábula de fuentes.
El tren y la mujer que llena el cielo.
Tu soledad esquiva en los hoteles
y tu máscara pura de otro signo.
Es la niñez del mar y tu silencio
donde los sabios vidrios se quebraban.
Es tu yerta ignorancia donde estuvo
mi torso limitado por el fuego.
Norma de amor te di, hombre de Apolo,
llanto con ruiseñor enajenado,
pero, pasto de ruina, te afilabas
para los breves sueños indecisos.
Pensamiento de enfrente, luz de ayer,
índices y señales del acaso.
Tu cintura de arena sin sosiego
atiende sólo rastros que no escalan.
Pero yo he de buscar por los rincones
tu alma tibia sin ti que no te entiende,
con el dolor de Apolo detenido
con que he roto la máscara que llevas.
Allí león, allí, furia del cielo,
te dejaré pacer en mis mejillas;
allí, caballo azul de mi locura,
pulso de nebulosa y minutero,
he de buscar las piedras de alacranes
y los vestidos de tu madre niña,
llanto de media noche y paño roto
que quitó luna de la sien del muerto.
Sí, tu niñez ya fábula de fuentes.
Alma extraña de mi hueco de venas,
te he de buscar pequeña y sin raíces.

YOUR CHILDHOOD IN MENTON

Yes, your childhood, a fable for fountains now.
                                          —JORGE GUILLÉN

Yes, your childhood, a fable for fountains now.
The train and the lady who overflows heaven.
Your solitude, shy in hotels,
and your pure mask, in another sign.
It is the childhood of ocean and silence
where oracular glasses are broken;
your hard-bitten ignorance, where before
was my torso defined by a flame.
Love's pattern I gave you, Apollonian man,
the nightingale's rage, in a cry,
yet, pasture of ruin, you grew lean
on the brief and equivocal fantasies.
Yesterday's brightness, antagonist mind,
chance's notations and omens.
Your waist of irresolute sand
heeded only the footpaths that found no way upward.
Mine then to pursue you in corners,
your spirit's lukewarmness, that cannot construe you, still lacking
     you,
with the grief of a hobbled Apollo
by whose power I shatter the mask that you bear.
Here, lion, here, indignation of heaven,
come and crop grass on my cheekbones;
here, you blue horse of my mania,
you nebula's pulse-beat, you minute-hand,
it is mine to seek out the scorpion's stone
and the skirts of your little-girl mother,
midnight's lament and the raveling cloths
that moonlight unbinds on the brows of the dead.
Yes, your childhood, a fable for fountains now.
O alien spirit, from the void of my veins,
it is mine to pursue you, so slight and so rootless.

13

¡Amor de siempre, amor, amor de nunca!
¡Oh, sí! Yo quiero. ¡Amor, amor! Dejadme.
No me tapen la boca los que buscan
espigas de Saturno por la nieve
o castran animales por un cielo,
clínica y selva de la anatomía.
Amor, amor, amor. Niñez del mar.
Tu alma tibia sin ti que no te entiende.
Amor, amor, un vuelo de la corza
por el pecho sin fin de la blancura.
Y tu niñez, amor, y tu niñez.
El tren y la mujer que llena el cielo.
Ni tú, ni yo, ni el aire, ni las hojas.
Sí, tu niñez ya fábula de fuentes.

Beloved forever, and never beloved, love!
For indeed I desire it! Love—leave me in peace!
do not stop up my mouth, you who seek
Saturnalian wheat in the snow,
or unsex the created of heaven,
anatomy's groves and dispensaries.
Love! Love! A childhood of ocean!
Your spirit's lukewarmness, that cannot construe you, still lacking
    you.
Love! Love! A running of deer
through an infinite bosom of whiteness.
And your childhood, beloved, your childhood.
The train and the lady who overflows heaven.
Not you, nor myself, nor the wind, nor the leaves.
Yes, your childhood, now fable for fountains.

II *LOS NEGROS*

Para Ángel del Río

NORMA Y PARAÍSO DE LOS NEGROS

Odian la sombra del pájaro
sobre el pleamar de la blanca mejilla
y el conflicto de luz y viento
en el salón de la nieve fría.

Odian la flecha sin cuerpo,
el pañuelo exacto de la despedida,
la aguja que mantiene presión y rosa
en el gramíneo rubor de la sonrisa.

Aman el azul desierto,
las vacilantes expresiones bovinas,
la mentirosa luna de los polos,
la danza curva del agua en la orilla.

Con la ciencia del tronco y del rastro
llenan de nervios luminosos la arcilla
y patinan lúbricos por agua y arenas
gustando la amarga frescura de su milenaria saliva.

Es por el azul crujiente,
azul sin un gusano ni una huella dormida,
donde los huevos de avestruz quedan eternos
y deambulan intactas las lluvias bailarinas.

Es por el azul sin historia,
azul de una noche sin temor de día,
azul donde el desnudo del viento va quebrando
los camellos sonámbulos de las nubes vacías.

Es allí donde sueñan los torsos bajo la gula de la hierba.
Allí los corales empapan la desesperación de la tinta,
los durmientes borran sus perfiles bajo la madeja de los caracoles
y queda el hueco de la danza sobre las últimas cenizas.

16

II *THE NEGROES*

For Ángel del Río

PATTERN AND PARADISE OF NEGROES

Bird's shadow they hate
on the white cheek at floodtide,
contention of light and the wind
in the courts of cold snow.

The incorporeal arrow they hate,
departure's particular handkerchief,
the needle of pressures and roses
in the grass-grown flush of a smile.

They love uninhabited blue,
the fleeting, expressive bovine,
the perjuring moon of the poles
and the dance-curve of water on beaches.

Theirs, with the lore of the trunk and the bypath,
to flood all the radiant nerve-ends of clay,
skating wanton on water and sand
and tasting in bitter refreshment, their millennial spittle.

Into crackling blueness they go,
blueness untouched by the worm or the somnolent footprint,
where the ostrich's egg holds eternity
and the rains dance away, undiminished.

Through anonymous blueness,
blueness of night with no terror of dawn,
blue where the nude of the wind goes, disheveling
the sleepwalking camels in the hollowing cloud.

Here, in insatiable grass, the torsos lie dreaming.
Here the coral is drenched with an ink's desperation,
and the sleeper effaces his profile, in the skein of the snail,
and the waste of the dance on the ultimate cinders, remains.

17

EL REY DE HARLEM

Con una cuchara
arrancaba los ojos a los cocodrilos
y golpeaba el trasero de los monos.
Con una cuchara.

Fuego de siempre dormía en los pedernales
y los escarabajos borrachos de anís
olvidaban el musgo de las aldeas.

Aquel viejo cubierto de setas
iba al sitio donde lloraban los negros
mientras crujía la cuchara del rey
y llegaban los tanques de agua podrida.

Las rosas huían por los filos
de las últimas curvas del aire,
y en los montones de azafrán
los niños machacaban pequeñas ardillas
con un rubor de frenesí manchado.

Es preciso cruzar los puentes
y llegar al rubor negro
para que el perfume de pulmón
nos golpee las sienes con su vestido
de caliente piña.

Es preciso matar al rubio vendedor de aguardiente,
a todos los amigos de la manzana y de la arena,
y es necesario dar con los puños cerrados
a las pequeñas judías que tiemblan llenas de burbujas,
para que el rey de Harlem cante con su muchedumbre,
para que los cocodrilos duerman en largas filas
bajo el amianto de la luna,
y para que nadie dude de la infinita belleza
de los plumeros, los ralladores, los cobres y las cacerolas de las
    cocinas.

THE KING OF HARLEM

With a spoon
he gouged out the crocodile's eyes
and thumped on the monkey-rumps,
with a spoon.

Eternity's spark still slept in the flint
and the scarabs that tippled on anise
had forgotten the moss of the parish.

And that patriarch, covered with mushrooms,
went on to the place where the black men were weeping
while the king's ladle crackled
and the tanks of the pestilent water arrived.

Roses fled on the blades
of the last loops of air
and on hummocks of saffron
the little boys smashed little squirrels
in the flush of a soiled exaltation.

Yes: the bridge must be crossed
and the florid black found
if the perfume we bear in our lungs
is to strike, in its guises of peppery pine,
on our temples.

We must murder the yellow-haired hawkers of brandy
and the comrades of apple and sand;
we must batter with fistblows
the gone little jewesses, in a lather of bubbles:
for the king and his hosts must come singing from Harlem,
the crocodiles sleep in the great enfilades,
in a moon of asbestos,
so that none may discredit the infinite beauty
of the dusters, the graters, the kitchenware coppers and casseroles.

¡Ay, Harlem! ¡Ay, Harlem! ¡Ay, Harlem!
Na hay angustia comparable a tus rojos oprimidos,
a tu sangre estremecida dentro del eclipse oscuro,
a tu violencia granate sordomuda en la penumbra,
a tu gran rey prisionero, con un traje de conserje!

* * * * * * * * * *

Tenía la noche una hendidura y quietas salamandras de marfil.
Las muchachas americanas
llevaban niños y monedas en el vientre
y los muchachos se desmayaban en la cruz del desperezo.

Ellos son.
Ellos son los que beben el whisky de plata junto a los volcanes
y tragan pedacitos de corazón por las heladas montañas del oso.

Aquella noche el rey de Harlem con una durísima cuchara
arrancaba los ojos a los cocodrilos
y golpeaba el trasero de los monos.
Con una cuchara.
Los negros lloraban confundidos
entre paraguas y soles de oro,
los mulatos estiraban gomas, ansiosos de llegar al torso blanco,
y el viento empañaba espejos
y quebraba las venas de los bailarines.

Negros, Negros, Negros, Negros.

La sangre no tiene puertas en vuestra noche boca arriba.
No hay rubor. Sangre furiosa por debajo de las pieles,
viva en la espina del puñal y en el pecho de los paisajes,
bajo las pinzas y las retamas de la celeste luna de cáncer.

Sangre que busca por mil caminos muertes enharinadas y ceniza
        de nardo,
cielos yertos, en declive, donde las colonias de planetas
rueden por las playas con los objetos abandonados.

You Harlem! You Harlem! You Harlem!
No anguish to equal your thwarted vermilions,
your blood-shaken, darkened eclipses,
your garnet ferocity, deaf and dumb in the shadows,
your hobbled, great king in the janitor's suit.

*   *   *   *   *   *   *   *   *   *

Night opened a fissure; ivory salamanders were mute.
The American girls
carried children and coins in their bellies
and the boys lay inert on the cross of a yawn and stretched muscle.

Take note of them:
They drink silver whiskey within sight of volcanoes
and devour little slivers of heart on the frozen ascents of the bear.

King Harlem that night, with the hardest of spoons,
gouged out the crocodile's eyes
and thumped on the monkey-rumps.
With a spoon.
The black men, befuddled, went wailing,
between gold sun and umbrellas,
the mulattoes pulled rubber, impatient to gain a white torso,
and wind blurred the mirrors
and ruptured the veins of the dancers.

    Negroes, Negroes, Negroes, Negroes.

Blood has no doors in your night, lying face to the sky.
Nowhere a blush. But under the skins, blood is raging,
alive in the spine of a dagger and the breast of a landscape,
under the pincers and brackens of Cancer's heavenly moon.

Blood on its thousand pathways, seeking powder-meal deaths,
    ashes of spikenard,
skies fixed in a slant, where the planets' assemblages
toss on the beach with the castaway things.

21

Sangre que mira lenta con el rabo del ojo,
hecha de espartos exprimidos, néctares de subterráneos.
Sangre que oxida el alisio descuidado en una huella
y disuelve a las mariposas en los cristales de la ventana.

Es la sangre que viene, que vendrá
por los tejados y azoteas, por todas partes,
para quemar la clorofilia de las mujeres rubias,
para gemir al pie de las camas ante el insomnio de los lavabo
y estrellarse en una aurora de tabaco y bajo amarillo.

Hay que huir,
huir por las esquinas y encerrarse en los últimos pisos,
porque el tuétano del bosque penetrará por las rendijas
para dejar en vuestra carne una leve huella de eclipse
y una falsa tristeza de guante desteñido y rosa química.

    *   *   *   *   *   *   *   *   *   *

Es por el silencio sapientísimo
cuando los camareros y los cocineros y los que limpian con la lengua
las heridas de los millonarios
buscan al rey por las calles o en los ángulos del salitre.

Un viento sur de madera, oblicuo en el negro fango,
escupe a las barcas rotas y se clava puntillas en los hombros
un viento sur que lleva
colmillos, girasoles, alfabetos
y una pila de Volta con avispas ahogadas.

El olvido estaba expresado por tres gotas de tinta sobre e
    monóculo,
el amor por un solo rostro invisible a flor de piedra.
Médulas y corolas componían sobre las nubes
un desierto de tallos sin una sola rosa.

    *   *   *   *   *   *   *   *   *   *

A la izquierda, a la derecha, por el sur y por el norte,
se levanta el muro impasible

Blood that looks long, through a corner of eye,
blood pressed out of matweed, subterranean nectars.
Blood rusting the tracks of the negligent trade wind
and melting the moth on the panes.

Blood flows; and will flow
on the rooftops and sheds everywhere;
to burn off the chlorophyl blondes,
to sob at the foot of the bed by insomniac washbowls
and explode in a low-yellow dawn of tobacco.

Escape, since you must:
escape in the corners, hole up in the uppermost stories,
for a marrow of forests will enter the crevices
and leave in your flesh a tentative trail of eclipse,
mock mourning: the discoloring glove and the chemical rose.

* * * * * * * * * *

In the shrewdest of silences
go the cooks and the valets, and those who would cleanse with
     their tongues
the millionaire's wounds,
seeking a king in the streets, or on crossways of nitre.

A wooden south wind, atilt on black slime
spits upon boatwrecks and tacks down its shoulders;
a southerly wind bearing
alphabets, sunflowers, incisors,
a storage-cell powered with a smother of wasps.

Oblivion spoke in three ink-droppings spotting a monocle,
and love, in the lonely, invisible face, on the rind of a rock.
Medullas, corollas, contrived on the cloud
a rose-barren desert of stubble.

* * * * * * * * * *

To left and to right, southward, northward,
looms up the impassable wall

para el topo, la aguja del agua.
No busquéis, negros, su grieta
para hallar la máscara infinita.
Buscad el gran sol del centro
hechos una piña zumbadora.
El sol que se desliza por los bosques
seguro de no encontrar una ninfa,
el sol que destruye números y no ha cruzado nunca un sueño,
el tatuado sol que baja por el río
y muge seguido de caimanes.

Negros, Negros, Negros, Negros.

Jamás sierpe, ni cebra, ni mula
palidecieron al morir.
El leñador no sabe cuándo expiran
los clamorosos árboles que corta.
Aguardad bajo la sombra vegetal de vuestro rey
a que cicutas y cardos y ortigas turben postreras azoteas.

Entonces, negros, entonces, entonces,
podréis besar con frenesí las ruedas de las bicicletas,
poner parejas de microscopios en las cuevas de las ardillas
y danzar al fin, sin duda, mientras las flores erizadas
asesinan a nuestro Moisés casi en los juncos del cielo.

¡Ay, Harlem, disfrazada!
¡Ay, Harlem, amenazada por un gentío de trajes sin cabeza!
Me llega tu rumor,
me llega tu rumor atravesando troncos y ascensores,
a través de láminas grises
donde flotan tus automóviles cubiertos de dientes,
a través de los caballos muertos y los crímenes diminutos,
a través de tu gran rey desesperado
cuyas barbas llegan al mar.

for the mole and the water-jet.
Black man, never search in its cleft
the immemorial mask.
Seek out the great sun of the center,
be the hum in the cluster.
Sun gliding through groves
with no expectation of dryads,
sun that undoes all the numbers, yet never crossed over a dream,
sun dropping tattooed on the river,
hallooing, with crocodiles after.

Negroes, Negroes, Negroes, Negroes.

Never serpent or zebra or mule
That paled at death's imminence.
Not even the woodcutter knows
when the death of the thunderous tree he brings down is
        accomplished.
Abide in the vegetal shade of your king
till the hemlock and thistle and thorn rock the furthermost roofs.

Black man: only then, only then, only then
can you kiss out your frenzy on bicycle-wheels
or pair off the microscopes in the caves of the squirrels,
and assuredly dance out the dance while the flower-stems stiffen
and murder our Moses—almost into bulrushes' heaven.

You Harlem in masquerade!
You Harlem, whom torsos of street-clothing menace!
Your murmur has come to me,
your murmur has come over tree trunks and dumb-waiters,
over grey metal-plate
where float all your tooth-covered speed-cars,
across the dead horses and the petty offenses,
past your noble and desperate king
whose beard-lengths go down to the sea.

IGLESIA ABANDONADA

(Balada de la Gran Guerra)

Yo tenía un hijo que se llamaba Juan.
Yo tenía un hijo.
Se perdió por los arcos un viernes de todos los muertos.
Lo vi jugar en las últimas escaleras de la misa
y echaba un cubito de hojalata en el corazón del sacerdote.
He golpeado los ataúdes. ¡Mi hijo! ¡Mi hijo! ¡Mi hijo!
Saqué una pata de gallina por detrás de la luna y luego
comprendí que mi niña era un pez
por donde se alejan las carretas.
Yo tenía una niña.
Yo tenía un pez muerto bajo la ceniza de los incensarios.
Yo tenía un mar. ¿De qué? ¡Dios mío! ¡Un mar!
Subí a tocar las campanas, pero las frutas tenían gusanos
y las cerrillas apagadas
se comían los trigos de la primavera.
Yo vi la transparente cigüeña de alcohol
mondar las negras cabezas de los soldados agonizantes
y vi las cabañas de goma
donde giraban las copas llenas de lágrimas.
En las anémonas del ofertorio te encontraré, ¡corazón mío!,
cuando el sacerdote levante la mula y el buey con sus fuertes brazos
para espantar los sapos nocturnos que rondan los helados paisajes
      del cáliz.
Yo tenía un hijo que era un gigante,
pero los muertos son más fuertes y saben devorar pedazos de cielo.
Si mi niño hubiera sido un oso,
yo no temería el sigilo de los caimanes,
ni hubiese visto al mar amarrado a los árboles
para ser fornicado y herido por el tropel de los regimientos.
¡Si mi niño hubiera sido un oso!
Me envolveré sobre esta lona dura para no sentir el frío de los
      musgos.

ABANDONED CHURCH

(Ballad of the Great War)

I'd a son named John,
I'd a son.
He was lost in the arches on a deathday in Friday.
I saw him at play on the uppermost stair of the Mass,
launching a little tin scoop at the heart of the priest.
I knocked on the coffinlids. Son! My son! Oh, my son!
From the other side of the moon I pulled up a chicken-claw,
and knew I'd a fish for a daughter,
in the place where the wagons recede.
I'd a daughter.
I'd a dead fish in the ash of the censers.
I'd an ocean. What made of? Good lord—just an ocean!
I climbed up to ring all the bells, but found the fruit wormy
and smothering match-ends
had eaten spring wheat.
The transparent alcohol stork, then I saw,
trimming the blackening skulls of the dying recruits;
cabins of rubber
where circled the goblets of tears.
Dear heart—let me find you in Eucharist's gift of anemones
when the priest with the might of his arms lifts the ox and the ass
to frighten the night-toad that paces the chalice's snowscapes.
I'd a son, I'd a giant,
but the dead are the mightiest, they can rend bits of heaven.
Had my son been a bear,
I would never have feared for the crocodile's secret
nor gazed at a tree-tethered sea
to be ravished and bled by a rabble of troops.
Had my son been a bear!
I'll wrap in coarse canvas, nor endure the cold mosses.

Sé muy bien que me darán una manga o la corbata;
pero en el centro de la misa yo romperé el timón y entonces
vendrá a la piedra la locura de pingüinos y gaviotas
que harán decir a los que duermen y a los que cantan por las
        esquinas:
él tenía un hijo.
¡Un hijo! ¡Un hijo! Un hijo
que no era más que suyo, porque era su hijo!
¡Su hijo! ¡Su hijo! ¡Su hijo!

I know, with good cause, that they'll send me a shirtsleeve or
     necktie,
but I'll smash, on the core of the Mass, the rudder-post; then
the madness of penguins and seagulls will come down on the stone
and give words to the sleepers and those who intone on the street-
     corners:
he'd a son!
He'd a son! He'd a son! He'd a son!
his, and no other's, for his son was his own!
He'd a son! He'd a son! He'd a son!

III *CALLES Y SUEÑOS*

A Rafael R. Rapún

Un pájaro de papel en el pecho
dice que el tiempo de los besos no ha llegado.
—Vicente Aleixandre

DANZA DE LA MUERTE

El mascarón. ¡Mirad el mascarón!
¡Cómo viene del África a New York!

Se fueron los árboles de la pimienta,
los pequeños botones de fósforo.
Se fueron los camellos de carne desgarrada
y los valles de luz que el cisne levantaba con el pico.

Era el momento de las cosas secas,
de la espiga en el ojo y el gato laminado,
del óxido de hierro de los grandes puentes
y el definitivo silencio del corcho.

Era la gran reunión de los animales muertos,
traspasados por las espadas de la luz;
la alegría eterna del hipopótamo con las pezuñas de ceniza
y de la gacela con una siempreviva en la garganta.

En la marchita soledad sin onda
el abollado mascarón danzaba.
Medio lado del mundo era de arena,
mercurio y sol dormido el otro medio.

El mascarón. ¡Mirad el mascarón!
¡Arena, caimán y miedo sobre Nueva York!

* * * * * * * *

III   *STREETS AND DREAMS*

For Rafael R. Rapún

> *A paper bird in my breast*
> *Says it is not yet the season of kisses.*
> —Vicente Aleixandre

DANCE OF DEATH

The mask! Lo, the mask!
It moves toward New York out of Africa!

Gone, all the pepper-trees,
and the small buds of phosphor.
The clawed flesh of camels, gone,
and the valleys of light, aloft on the swan's bill.

Time for the parched things:
wheat taking the eye, cats flattened to sheet-metal;
the big bridge corroding in iron
and the definitive silence of cork.

For the massive assembly of the animal dead
transfixed by the light-blades,
the cinder-hooved hippo's inexhaustible joy,
the gazelle, immortelle in its throat.

Unrippled in withering solitude,
jigs the blow-bitten mask.
Half a planet was sand,
the other half, sun-drowse and quicksilver.

The mask! Lo, the mask!
Crocodile, panic, and sand on New York!

*   *   *   *   *   *   *   *

Desfiladeros de cal aprisionaban un cielo vacío
donde sonaban las voces de los que mueren bajo el guano.
Un cielo mondado y puro, idéntico a sí mismo,
con el bozo y lirio agudo de sus montañas invisibles,

acabó con los más leves tallitos del canto
y se fué al diluvio empaquetado de la savia,
a través del descanso de los últimos desfiles,
levantando con el rabo pedazos de espejo.

Cuando el chino lloraba en el tejado
sin encontrar el desnudo de su mujer
y el director del banco observaba el manómetro
que mide el cruel silencio de la moneda,
el mascarón llegaba al Wall Street.

No es extraño para la danza
este columbario que pone los ojos amarillos.
De la esfinge a la caja le caudales hay un hilo tenso
que atraviesa el corazón de todos los niños pobres.
El ímpetu primitivo baila con el ímpetu mecánico,
ignorantes en su frenesí de la luz original.
Porque si la rueda olvida su fórmula,
ya puede cantar desnuda con las manadas de caballos;
y si una llama quema los helados proyectos,
el cielo tendrá que huir ante el tumulto de las ventanas.

No es extraño este sitio para la danza, yo lo digo.
El mascarón bailará entre columnas de sangre y de números,
entre huracanes de oro y gemidos de obreros parados
que aullarán, noche oscura, por tu tiempo sin luces,
¡oh salvaje Norteamérica! ¡oh impúdica! ¡oh salvaje,
tendida en la frontera de la nieve!

El mascarón. ¡Mirad el mascarón!
¡Qué ola de fango y luciérnaga sobre Nueva York!

*   *   *   *   *   *   *   *

Causeways of lime held the hollow sky captive,
and voices of dead men were heard under guano.
Sky, equalling only itself, immaculate, scoured,
with the salient lily and the down of invisible summits—

Done with the airiest tendrils of song,
and gone on the deluge that thickens the sap,
through the calm of the last of the marching formations,
lifting a mirrory rubble of glass on its tail.

When the Chinaman wept on the roof
because the nudeness of woman escaped him,
when the banker examined the pressure-gauge
and computed the merciless silence of money
the mask was at Wall Street.

Not unknown to that dance
the gold-eyed columbarium.
From the sphinx to the treasure-vault runs the tightening thread
that pierces the children of want to the heart.
Mechanical impulse and primitive urge dance as one
and forget, in their frenzy, the light of creation.
Could the wheel but unlearn its conformity
it might sing with the herd of the horses, untrammeled,
and should a flame scorch the frozen agendas,
all heaven would flee from the tumult of windows.

The place is not strange to the dance; be assured.
Between columns of numbers and blood, the mask cuts its figure,
between tempests of gold and the groans of the jobless
howling the epoch's extinction of light, in nighttime's obscurity,
O savage and shameless America! Savage
supine on your snowy frontiers!

The mask! Lo, the mask!
Firefly and slime in wave upon wave in New York!

* * * * * * * *

Yo estaba en la terraza luchando con la luna.
Enjambres de ventanas acribillaban un muslo de la noche.
En mis ojos bebían las dulces vacas de los cielos.
Y las brisas de largos remos
golpeaban los cenicientos cristales de Broadway.

La gota de sangre buscaba la luz de la yema del astro
para fingir una muerta semilla de manzana.
El aire de la llanura, empujado por los pastores,
temblaba con un miedo de molusco sin concha.

Pero no son los muertos los que bailan,
estoy seguro.
Los muertos están embebidos, devorando sus propias manos.
Son los otros los que bailan con el mascarón y su vihuela;
son los otros, los borrachos de plata, los hombres fríos,
los que crecen en el cruce de los muslos y llamas duras,
los que buscan la lombriz en el paisaje de las escaleras,
los que beben en el banco lágrimas de niña muerta
o los que comen por las esquinas diminutas pirámides del alba.

¡Que no baile el Papa!
¡No, que no baile el Papa!
Ni el Rey,
ni el millonario de dientes azules,
ni las bailarinas secas de las catedrales,
ni constructores, ni esmeraldas, ni locos, ni sodomitas.
Sólo este mascarón,
este mascarón de vieja escarlatina,
¡sólo este mascarón!

Que ya las cobras silbarán por los últimos pisos,
que ya las ortigas estremecerán patios y terrazas,
que ya la Bolsa será una pirámide de musgo,
que ya vendrán lianas después de los fusiles
y muy pronto, muy pronto, muy pronto.
¡Ay, Wall Street!

I strove with the moon on the terrace.
Window swarms riddled a thigh of the night.
Heaven's mild heifers drank their fill at my eyes,
and gusts of great wings
smote the window-glass hearth-beds of Broadway.

A blood-drop was seeking the light at the quick of a star
to dissemble dead apple-pips.
A wind from the plains, urged on by shepherds,
shook with the fear of the mollusc-shell, open.

But the dead do not dance.
I am persuaded of that.
The dead keep their distance, gnawing away at their fingers.
Others must dance with the Mask and the Masquer's guitar:
others, the drunkards of silver, the frigid ones,
those who thrive in the crotch of a thigh and hard flame,
those who follow the worm in a landscape of ladders,
those who drink down the tears of dead girls in the bank-lobby
or eat the pyramidal crumbs of the dawn on the corners.

No dance for His Holiness!
No dancing at all for His Eminence!
And none for the King,
and none for the blue-dentured millionaire,
or the stale temple-dancers,
or contractors, or emeralds, or madmen, or sodomites.
Only the mask!
the mask of worn scarlet,
there is only the mask!

Time for the cobras to hiss on the uppermost levels,
for the nettle to jostle the patios and roof-gardens,
for the Market to crash in a pyramid of moss,
time for the jungle lianas that follow the rifles—
soon, soon enough, ever so soon.
Woe to you, Wall Street!

El mascarón. ¡Mirad el mascarón!
¡Cómo escupe veneno de bosque
por la angustia imperfecta de Nueva York!

Diciembre 1929

The mask! Lo, the mask!
Spitting wilderness venom
over New York's imperfect despair!

December 1929

PAISAJE DE LA MULTITUD QUE VOMITA

(Anochecer de Coney Island)

La mujer gorda venía delante
arrancando las raíces y mojando el pergamino· de los tambores;
la mujer gorda
que vuelve del revés los pulpos agonizantes.
La mujer gorda, enemiga de la luna,
corría por las calles y los pisos deshabitados
y dejaba por los rincones pequeñas calaveras de paloma
y levantaba las furias de los banquetes de los siglos últimos
y llamaba al demonio del pan por las colinas del cielo barrido
y filtraba un ansia de luz en las circulaciones subterráneas.
Son los cementerios, lo sé, son los cementerios
y el dolor de las cocinas enterradas bajo la arena,
son los muertos, los faisanes y las manzanas de otra hora
los que nos empujan en la garganta.

Llegaban los rumores de la selva del vómito
con las mujeres vacías, con niños de cera caliente,
con árboles fermentados y camareros incansables
que sirven platos de sal bajo las arpas de la saliva.
Sin remedio, hijo mío, ¡vomita! No hay remedio.
No es el vómito de los húsares sobre los pechos de la prostituta,
ni el vómito del gato que se tragó una rana por descuido.
Son los muertos que arañan con sus manos de tierra
las puertas de pedernal donde se pudren nublos y postres.

La mujer gorda venía delante
con las gentes de los barcos, de las tabernas y de los jardines,
El vómito agitaba delicadamente sus tambores
entre algunas niñas de sangre
que pedían protección a la luna.
¡Ay de mí! ¡Ay de mí! ¡Ay de mí!
Esta mirada mía fué mía, pero ya no es mía,
esta mirada que tiembla desnuda por el alcohol

LANDSCAPE OF THE VOMITING MULTITUDES

(Coney Island Dusk)

The fat lady came on,
pulling up roots and wetting the drum-skins;
the fat lady
who turns up the cuttlefish and leaves them to die, wrong side out.
The fat lady, hostile to moons,
raced through the streets and the tenantless levels,
leaving pigeon-skull trails in the corners,
kindling the furies of obsolete feasts,
calling the demon of bread from the slopes of swept sky
and sifting light's ardor into underground transits.
They are graveyards. I know it. They are graveyards,
a sadness of kitchens sunk deep under silt;
another time's pheasants and apples; those who tighten our throats
are the dead.

A muttering came from the forest of vomit:
woman's sterility, molten-wax children,
fermentation of trees, and unwearying waiters
serving platters of salt under harps of saliva.
No help for it! Vomit it up, boy! No other way.
Not the vomit of hussars on the breasts of their harlots,
or the vomit of cats unmindfully gulping down frogs.
Those who scratch with the clay of their hands
on the doorways of flint and the rotting confections and clouds,
    are the dead.

The fat lady came on
with the crowds from the boats and the bars and the gardens.
The fanfare was light on the drumheads of vomit
by the daughters of blood
who seek the protection of moons.
Welladay! Welladay! Welladay!
My gaze, that was one time my own, is no longer my own,
a gaze trembling naked in alcohol,

y despide barcos increíbles
por las anémonas de los muelles.
Me defiendo con esta mirada
que mana de las ondas por donde el alba no se atreve,
yo, poeta sin brazos, perdido
entre la multitud que vomita,
sin caballo efusivo que corte
los espesos musgos de mis sienes.

Pero la mujer gorda seguía delante
y la gente buscaba las farmacias
donde el amargo trópico se fija.
Sólo cuando izaron la bandera y llegaron los primeros canes
la ciudad entera se agolpó en las barandillas del embarcadero.

Nueva York, 29 de diciembre de 1929

launching incredible navies
on quays of anemone.
The gaze that preserves me
must issue on waves where dawn never ventures:
I, poet and armless, adrift
in the vomiting multitudes,
lacking even the spirit of horses to crop
the rank moss of my temples.

But the fat lady came on, as before,
and the crowds called for druggists
where the tropical bitters were waiting.
And not till the first curs arrived, and they broke out the flags,
did the city swarm out to the rails of the jetty, as one.

New York, December 29, 1929

PAISAJE DE LA MULTITUD QUE ORINA

(Nocturno de Battery Place)

Se quedaron solos:
aguardaban la velocidad de las últimas bicicletas.
Se quedaron solas:
esperaban la muerte de un niño en el velero japonés.
Se quedaron solos y solas
soñando con los picos abiertos de los pájaros agonizantes,
con el agudo quitasol que pincha
al sapo recién aplastado,
bajo un silencio con mil orejas
y diminutas bocas de agua
en los desfiladeros que resisten
el ataque violento de la luna.
Lloraba el niño del velero y se quebraban los corazones
angustiados por el testigo y la vigilia de todas las cosas
y porque todavía en el suelo celeste de negras huellas
gritaban nombres oscuros, salivas y radios de níquel.
No importa que el niño calle cuando le clavan el último alfiler,
no importa la derrota de la brisa en la corola del algodón,
porque hay un mundo de la muerte con marineros definitivos
que se asomarán a los arcos y os helarán por detrás de los árboles.
Es inútil buscar el recodo
donde la noche olvida su viaje
y acechar un silencio que no tenga
trajes rotos y cáscaras y llanto,
porque tan sólo el diminuto banquete de la araña
basta para romper el equilibrio de todo el cielo.
No hay remedio para el gemido del velero japonés,
ni para estas gentes ocultas que tropiezan con las esquinas.
El campo se muerde la cola para unir las raíces en un punto
y el ovillo busca por la grama su ansia de longitud insatisfecha.
¡La luna! Los policías. ¡Las sirenas de los trasatlánticos!
Fachadas de crin, de humo; anémonas, guantes de goma.

LANDSCAPE OF THE URINATING MULTITUDES

(BATTERY PLACE NOCTURNE)

They kept to themselves, being men,
and awaited the rush of the ultimate cyclists.
They kept to themselves, being women,
and awaited the death of a boy on a Japanese cutter.
Men and women: they kept to themselves,
dreaming the death of the birds, with mouths open like birds,
pricking with parasol points
the toad lately gutted
in a thousand-eared silence
by the outlets of water
in defiles that resist
the raging assault of the moon.
The boy in the cutter wept on, there was breaking of hearts,
in the anguish that broods on the vigil and witness of things
and the marvel that always in a heavenly marl of dark footfalls,
dim names cry out spittle and nickel-plate radios.
And what if the boy, when the last nail goes in, is quiet?
And what if a breeze is concealed in the cotton's corolla?
We remain in a world of the dead, with definitive sailors
that peer from the arches and curdle your blood behind trees.
Useless to look for the bend
where night misses the way
or ambush a silence that wants
a rag of torn clothing, a husk, or a cry;
for the spider's diminutive banquet suffices
to shatter the balance of heaven.
No help for the moan from the Japanese cutter
or the secretive stumblers on street-corners.
The field bites its tail to assemble its roots in a place
and the raddle of yarn in the grass seeks a length of ungratified
    ardor.
The moon! The police! Klaxons across the Atlantic!
False fronts of horsehair and smoke; rubber gloves and anemones.

Todo está roto por la noche,
abierta de piernas sobre las terrazas.
Todo está roto por los tibios caños
de una terrible fuente silenciosa.
¡Oh gentes! ¡Oh mujercillas! ¡Oh soldados!
Será preciso viajar por los ojos de los idiotas,
campos libres donde silban mansas cobras deslumbradas,
paisajes llenos de sepulcros que producen fresquísimas manzanas,
para que venga la luz desmedida
que temen los ricos detrás de sus lupas,
el olor de un solo cuerpo con la doble vertiente de lis y rata
y para que se quemen estas gentes que pueden orinar alrededor de
      un gemido
o en los cristales donde se comprenden las olas nunca repetidas.

All wrecked in the night,
legs sprawled on the terraces.
All wrecked in warm gutterpipes
and a terrible silence of fountains.
Good people! Soldiers and wantons!
The journey must lead through the idiot's eye,
cross-country, to the hiss of the dazed and the housebroken cobras,
landscapes of graveyards that foster the ruddiest apples.
For light without limit must fall,
and the well-to-do looking through lenses
quake at the smell of a body whose gradient doubles the rat and the
    lily;
where those who encircle a groan with a spilling of urine
or the crystals withholding the never-repetitive wave,
must be utterly given to flame.

ASESINATO

—*¿Cómo fué?*
—Una grieta en la mejilla.
¡Eso es todo!
Una uña que aprieta el tallo.
Un alfiler que bucea
hasta encontrar las raicillas del grito.
Y el mar deja de moverse.
—*¿Cómo, cómo fué?*
—Así.
—*¡Déjame! ¿De esa manera?*
—Sí.
El corazón salió solo.
—*¡Ay, ay de mí!*

MURDER

(Riverside Drive: Two Voices At Dawn)

"What happened?"
"A slash on the cheek
Nothing more!
A thorn-point to harass a stalk.
A pinprick to dive
till it touches the roots of a cry.
And the sea moves no more."
"What happened? What happened?"
"It was this way."
"Stand aside! Was it this way?"
"Yes, this way.
Only a heart going out."
"Heaven help me!"

NAVIDAD EN EL HUDSON

¡Esa esponja gris!
Ese marinero recién degollado.
Ese río grande.
Esa brisa de límites oscuros.
Ese filo, amor, ese filo.
Estaban los cuatro marineros luchando con el mundo,
con el mundo de aristas que ven todos los ojos,
con el mundo que no se puede recorrer sin caballos.
Estaban uno, cien, mil marineros,
luchando con el mundo de las agudas velocidades,
sin enterarse de que el mundo
estaba solo por el cielo.

El mundo solo por el cielo solo.
Son las colinas de martillos y el triunfo de la hierba espesa.
Son los vivísimos hormigueros y las monedas en el fango.
El mundo solo por el cielo solo
y el aire a la salida de todas las aldeas.

Cantaba la lombriz el terror de la rueda
y el marinero degollado
cantaba el oso de agua que lo había de estrechar;
y todos cantaban aleluya,
aleluya. Cielo desierto.
Es lo mismo, ¡lo mismo!, aleluya.

He pasado toda la noche en los andamios de los arrabales
dejándome la sangre por la escayola de los proyectos,
ayudando a los marineros a recoger las velas desgarradas.
Y estoy con las manos vacías en el rumor de la desembocadura.
No importa que cada minuto
un niño nuevo agite sus ramitos de venas,
ni que el parto de la víbora, desatado bajo las ramas,
calme la sed de sangre de los que miran el desnudo.
Lo que importa es esto: hueco. Mundo solo. Desembocadura.

CHRISTMAS ON THE HUDSON

This gray sponge:
this sea-farer, lately beheaded!
This mighty river.
This wind from the shadowy zenith.
And this cutting-edge, love, this cutting edge!
Four sailors wrestled a planet,
a world of discernible angles,
an uncrossable world, save by horses.
One sailor, one hundred, one thousand,
wrestling the critical speeds of a planet,
and unaware, all of them,
that the world was alone in the sky.

A planet alone in a heaven alone.
With hammer-head hills and the grasses' rank mastery.
With ravening ant heaps, coins in the slime.
A planet alone in a heaven alone
and wind at the village's outskirts.

The earthworm sang of the terror of wheels
and the sailor, lately beheaded,
sang of the crush of the water-bear fated to hold him;
and all sang together: alleluia,
alleluia! O desolate heaven!
All one! All one! Allelulia!

All night I stood on the gangplanks of suburbs,
letting blood on the stucco of blueprints
and worked with the sailors who battened the tatters of canvas.
Am now at the murmuring mouth of the river, empty-handed.
What matter if, prompt to the minute,
the newly-born shake out the branch of their veins,
or the offspring of vipers uncoiling on boughs,
calm the blood-thirsty voyeurs of nakedness.
What matters is only: the void. A planet alone. An outlet of
    harbor.

49

Alba no. Fábula inerte.
Sólo esto: Desembocadura.
¡Oh esponja mía gris!
¡Oh cuello mío recién degollado!
¡Oh río grande mío!
¡Oh brisa mía de límites que no son míos!
¡Oh filo de mi amor, oh hiriente filo!

Nueva York, 27 de diciembre de 1929

And never a dawn. O preposterous fable!
This then: an outlet of harbor.
Gray sponge: which is mine!
The neck newly severed: which is mine.
The great river: mine.
The wind from the zenith that can never be mine: which is mine.
And my love's cutting-edge. O wound-working edge!

New York, December 27, 1929

CIUDAD SIN SUEÑO

(Nocturno del Brooklyn Bridge)

No duerme nadie por el cielo. Nadie, nadie.
No duerme nadie.
Las criaturas de la luna huelen y rondan sus cabañas.
Vendrán las iguanas vivas a morder a los hombres que no sueñan
y el que huye con el corazón roto encontrará por las esquinas
al increíble cocodrilo quieto bajo la tierna protesta de los astros.

No duerme nadie por el mundo. Nadie, nadie.
No duerme nadie.
Hay un muerto en el cementerio más lejano
que se queja tres años
porque tiene un paisaje seco en la rodilla;
y el niño que enterraron esta mañana lloraba tanto
que hubo necesidad de llamar a los perros para que callase.

No es sueño la vida. ¡Alerta! ¡Alerta! ¡Alerta!
Nos caemos de las escaleras para comer la tierra húmeda
o subimos al filo de la nieve con el coro de las dalias muertas.
Pero no hay olvido, ni sueño:
carne viva. Los besos atan las bocas
en una maraña de venas recientes
y al que le duele su dolor le dolerá sin descanso
y al que teme la muerte la llevará sobre sus hombros.

Un día
los caballos vivirán en las tabernas
y las hormigas furiosas
atacarán los cielos amarillos que se refugian en los ojos de las vacas.

Otro día
veremos la resurrección de las mariposas disecadas
y aún andando por un paisaje de esponjas grises y barcos mudos
veremos brillar nuestro anillo y manar rosas de nuestra lengua.

UNSLEEPING CITY
(Brooklyn Bridge Nocturne)

No sleep in the sky; nobody, nobody.
No one lies sleeping.
The spawn of the moon sniff the cabins, and circle.
The living iguanas arrive and set tooth on the sleepless.
The heartstricken one who takes flight will meet on the corners
the incredible mute crocodile under the timid reproach of the
    stars.

No sleep upon earth; nobody, nobody.
No one lies sleeping.
The corpse in the furthermost graveyard
that was three years berating
the landscape of drought that he held on his knees,
and the boy that they buried this morning—he whimpered so
    much
they called out the mastiffs to quiet him.

Life is no dream! Beware and beware and beware!
We tumble downstairs to eat of the damp of the earth
or we climb to the snowy divide with the choir of dead dahlias.
But neither dream nor forgetfulness, is:
brute flesh is. Kisses that tether our mouths
in a mesh of raw veins.
Whomsoever his woe brings to grief, it will grieve without quarter.
Whom death brings to dread will carry that death on his
    shoulders.

On a day,
the horses will thrive in the taverns,
the ravening ant
will assail yellow heavens withheld in the eyes of a cow.

On a time
we shall see, rearisen, the anatomized butterflies,
and walking the ways of gray sponge and a stillness of boats,
behold our rings glisten and the roses gush forth from our tongues.

¡Alerta! ¡Alerta! ¡Alerta!
A los que guardan todavía huellas de zarpa y aguacero,
a aquel muchacho que llora porque no sabe la invención del puente
o a aquel muerto que ya no tiene más que la cabeza y un zapato,
hay que llevarlos al muro donde iguanas y sierpes esperan,
donde espera la dentadura del oso,
donde espera la mano momificada del niño
y la piel del camello se eriza con un violento escalofrío azul.

No duerme nadie por el cielo. Nadie, nadie.
No duerme nadie.
Pero si alguien cierra los ojos,
¡azotadlo, hijos míos, azotadlo!
Haya un panorama de ojos abiertos
y amargas llagas encendidas.
No duerme nadie por el mundo. Nadie, nadie.
Ya lo he dicho.
No duerme nadie.
Pero si alguien tiene por la noche exceso de musgo en las sienes
abrid los escotillones para que vea bajo la luna
las copas falsas, el veneno y la calavera de los teatros.

Beware and beware and beware!
Those still keeping watch on the print of the paw and the
    cloudburst,
the boy in his tears, who cannot interpret the bridge's invention,
the dead with no more than a head and a shoe now—
drive them all to the wall where snake and iguana are waiting,
where the bear's fang lies ready
and the mummified hand of the child
and the pelt of the camel in a raging blue ague, stands on end.

No sleep under heaven; nobody, nobody.
No one lies sleeping.
And should one shut an eye,
lay on the whip, my boys, lay on the whip!
Let eye's panorama be open, I say,
let the bitter sores rankle!
No sleep upon earth; nobody, nobody,
no one, I tell you.
No one lies sleeping.
But if any should find in the night the mosses' excess on his
    temples—
down with the trapdoors and let there be seen in the moon
the perfidious goblets, the theater's skull, and the bane.

PANORAMA CIEGO DE NUEVA YORK

Si no son los pájaros
cubiertos de ceniza,
si no son los gemidos que golpean las ventanas de la boda,
serán las delicadas criaturas del aire
que manan la sangre nueva por la oscuridad inextinguible.
Pero no, no son los pájaros,
porque los pájaros están a punto de ser bueyes;
pueden ser rocas blancas con la ayuda de la luna
y son siempre muchachos heridos
antes de que los jueces levanten la tela.

Todos comprenden el dolor que se relaciona con la muerte,
pero el verdadero dolor no está presente en el espíritu.
No está en el aire ni en nuestra vida,
ni en estas terrazas llenas de humo.
El verdadero dolor que mantiene despiertas las cosas
es una pequeña quemadura infinita
en los ojos inocentes de los otros sistemas.

Un traje abandonado pesa tanto en los hombros
que muchas veces el cielo los agrupa en ásperas manadas.
Y las que mueren de parto saben en la última hora
que todo rumor será piedra y toda huella latido.
Nosotros ignoramos que el pensamiento tiene arrabales
donde el filósofo es devorado por los chinos y las orugas.
Y algunos niños idiotas han encontrado por las cocinas
pequeñas golondrinas con muletas
que sabían pronunciar la palabra amor.

No, no son los pájaros.
No es un pájaro el que expresa la turbia fiebre de laguna,
ni el ansia de asesinato que nos oprime cada momento,
ni el metálico rumor de suicidio que nos anima cada madrugada
Es una cápsula de aire donde nos duele todo el mundo,

BLIND PANORAMA OF NEW YORK

If not birds,
covered with ashes,
if not cries beating the bridegroom's windows,
they are delicate creatures of air
oozing fresh blood in unquenchable darkness.
But these are no birds,
for almost the bird metamorphosed, is ox;
white boulders, perhaps, with the help of a moon—
but always the stabbed adolescent
awaiting the judges' approach and the lifting of cloth.

The kinships of woe and mortality, we know,
but grief absolute is not given to spirit.
Not air, nor our lifetime's duration,
nor the smoke-laden terrace retains it.
Grief absolute, grief of the wakened awareness of things,
is a part of eternity's burning,
in the eyes of the guilelessly onlooking systems.

So heavy the weight of the castaway cloth on our shoulders
that sometimes the firmament packs them in hard constellations.
Those dead in their birth-pangs understand, in the last hour of all,
that all utterance is stone and each footfall, convulsion.
Ours never to know meditation's frontiers
where larvae and mandarin devour the philosopher.
And idiot children discover in kitchens
little swallows on crutches
adept in the single word: love.

These are no birds.
Bird cannot encompass the fever and murk of lagoons
nor the murderous dread that oppresses us, moment by moment,
nor metallic reports of self-slaughter that quicken us, morning by
    morning.
What stays, is a capsule of air where we groan on the rack of the
    world,

es un pequeño espacio vivo al loco unisón de la luz,
es una escala indefinible donde las nubes y rosas olvidan
el griterío chino que bulle por el desembarcadero de la sangre.
Yo muchas veces me he perdido
para buscar la quemadura que mantiene despiertas las cosas
y sólo he encontrado marineros echados sobre las barandillas
y pequeñas criaturas del cielo enterradas bajo la nieve.
Pero el verdadero dolor estaba en otras plazas
donde los peces cristalizados agonizaban dentro de los troncos,
plazas del cielo extraño para las antiguas estatuas ilesas
y para la tierna intimidad de los volcanes.

No hay dolor en la voz. Sólo existen los dientes,
pero dientes que callarán aislados por el raso negro.
No hay dolor en la voz. Aquí sólo existe la Tierra.
La tierra con sus puertas de siempre
que llevan al rubor de los frutos.

an interval warm to the lunatic fusion of light,
an equivocal scale where the clouds and the roses forget
Chinese pandemonium that boils through an outlet of blood.
Oftentimes I have lost myself wholly
on the track of the burning that wakens awareness of things,
and found only the sailor, tossed on the taffrail,
and the skies' little creatures lying buried in snow.
But woe absolute was always a village square distant,
where crystallized fish perished under the tree trunk;
courtyards of sky unknown to the statue's unblemished antiquity,
and the tender advance of volcanoes.

No woe in our voices. Only the teeth, set,
teeth to be stilled in a fold of black satin.
No woe in our voices. Here only our planet persists.
Our earth, with its gates of forever,
that give on the flush of its fruits.

NACIMIENTO DE CRISTO

Un pastor pide teta por la nieve que ondula
blancos perros tendidos entre linternas sordas.
El Cristito de barro se ha partido los dedos
en los filos eternos de la madera rota.

¡Ya vienen las hormigas y los pies ateridos!
Dos hilillos de sangre quiebran el cielo duro.
Los vientres del demonio resuenan por los valles
golpes y resonancias de carne de molusco.

Lobos y sapos cantan en las hogueras verdes
coronadas por vivos hormigueros del alba.
La mula tiene un sueño de grandes abanicos
y el toro sueña un toro de agujeros y de agua.

El niño llora y mira con un tres en la frente.
San José ve en el heno tres espinas de bronce.
Los pañales exhalan un rumor de desierto
con cítaras sin cuerdas y degolladas voces.

La nieve de Manhatan empuja los anuncios
y lleva gracia pura por las falsas ojivas.
Sacerdotes idiotas y querubes de pluma
van detrás de Lutero por las altas esquinas.

BIRTH OF CHRIST

A shepherd gropes for the nipple in a snowdrift that tosses
white dogs by the swaddle of lanterns, recumbent.
The little clay christus has chipped off its fingers and toes
on a knife-edge eternally bared in the splintering wood.

Time for the ants' visitations and the frost-stiffened foot!
Two little cross-threads of blood break the hardness of heaven.
In the valleys, the entrails of demons redouble
the strokes and the resonance heard in the meat of the mollusc.

The wolf sings with the toad in a green conflagration
crowned with the ravening anthills of morning.
The mule dozes off in a dream, the enormous fans of a dream,
and the bull dreams a bull pierced with pot-holes and water.

The child, with a 3 on his forehead, laments and looks on.
St. Joseph sees in the hay three thorn-points of bronze.
The swaddling clout falls in the breath of a wilderness murmur,
and zithers with keyboards unstrung, and headless ones singing,
      are heard.

Snow in Manhattan weighs down the billboards
and bears its immaculate grace up the fraudulent arches.
The idiot priest and the feathering host of the cherubim
move on, in the lofty arcades, after Luther.

LA AURORA

La Aurora de Nueva York tiene
cuatro columnas de cieno
y un huracán de negras palomas
que chapotean las aguas podridas.

La aurora de Nueva York gime
por las inmensas escaleras
buscando entre las aristas
nardos de angustia dibujada.

La aurora llega y nadie la recibe en su boca
porque allí no hay mañana ni esperanza posible.
A veces las monedas en enjambres furiosos
taladran y devoran abandonados niños.

Los primeros que salen comprenden con sus huesos
que no habrá paraíso ni amores deshojados;
saben que van al cieno de números y leyes,
a los juegos sin arte, a sudores sin fruto.

La luz es sepultada por cadenas y ruidos
en impúdico reto de ciencia sin raíces.
Por los barrios hay gentes que vacilan insomnes
como recién salidas de un naufragio de sangre.

DAWN

Dawn in New York bears
four pillars of slime
and a storm of black pigeons
that dabble dead water.

Dawn in New York grieves
on the towering stairs
seeking on ledges
pangs traced upon nard.

Dawn comes, there is no mouth to receive it,
for here neither morning nor promise is possible.
Only now and again a furious rabble of coins
that enter and ravage the dispossessed childhoods.

The first on the streets know the truth in their bones:
for these, neither Eden, nor passions unleafing;
they go to the slough of the ciphers and strictures,
to the games without genius and the sweat without profit.

Light is buried in chains and alarums
in the menace of science, rootless and impudent.
And staggering there in the suburbs, the insomniacs,
as though lately escaped from a bloody disaster.

IV *POEMAS DEL LAGO EDEM MILLS*

A Eduardo Ugarte

POEMA DOBLE DEL LAGO EDEM*

Nuestro ganado pace, el viento espira.
—GARCILASO

Era mi voz antigua
ignorante de los densos jugos amargos.
La adivino lamiendo mis pies
bajo los frágiles helechos mojados.

¡Ay voz antigua de mi amor,
ay voz de mi verdad,
ay voz de mi abierto costado,
cuando todas las rosas manaban de mi lengua
y el césped no conocía la impassible dentadura del caballo!

Estás aquí bebiendo mi sangre,
bebiendo mi humor de niño pesado,
mientras mis ojos se quiebran en el viento
con el aluminio y las voces de los borrachos.

Déjame pasar la puerta
donde Eva come hormigas
y Adán fecunda peces deslumbrados.
Déjame pasar, hombrecillo de los cuernos,
al bosque de los desperezos
y los alegrísimos saltos.

Yo sé el uso más secreto
que tiene un viejo alfiler oxidado
y sé del horror de unos ojos despiertos
sobre la superficie concreta del plato.

* In Lorca's letter to Ángel del Río, the name is correctly given as Eden Mills.

IV   *POEMS FROM LAKE EDEN MILLS*

For Eduardo Ugarte

DOUBLE POEM OF LAKE EDEN

Our herd is grazing, the wind breathes.
—GARCILASO

It was another time's voice,
unskilled in the flow of the thick and the bitter.
I foresaw it, lapping my feet
under dampened and delicate fern.

Another time's voice of my love,
voice of my candor,
voice of my opening side,
when my tongue ran with roses
and the turf never knew the indifferent tooth of the horse.

Here you come, drinking my blood,
drinking the cumbersome humors of childhood,
while my eyes in the wind splinter
on voices of drunkards and aluminum.

Let me pass by that gate
where Eve gnaws the ant
and Adam impregnates a dazzle of fish.
Give way to me, horned little man, let me pass
to the grove of the loose-limbed
and the outleaping happiest.

I know all the recondite uses
of the rusting old blade
and the horror of wakening eyes
on the concrete expanse of the salver.

Pero no quiero mundo ni sueño, voz divina,
quiero mi libertad, mi amor humano
en el rincón más oscuro de la brisa que nadie quiera.
¡Mi amor humano!

Esos perros marinos se persiguen
y el viento acecha troncos descuidados.
¡Oh voz antigua, quema con tu lengua
esta voz de hojalata y de talco!

Quiero llorar porque me da la gana
como lloran los niños del último banco,
porque yo no soy un hombre, ni un poeta, ni una hoja,
pero sí un pulso herido que sonda las cosas del otro lado.

Quiero llorar diciendo mi nombre,
rosa, niño y abeto a la orilla de este lago,
para decir mi verdad de hombre de sangre
matando en mí la burla y la sugestión del vocablo.

No, no, yo no pregunto, yo deseo,
voz mía libertada que me lames las manos.
En el laberinto de biombos es mi desnudo el que recibe
la luna de castigo y el reloj encenizado.

Así hablaba yo.
Así hablaba yo cuando Saturno detuvo los trenes
y la bruma y el sueño y la muerte me estaban buscando.
Me estaban buscando
allí donde mugen las vacas que tienen patitas de paje
y allí donde flota mi cuerpo entre los equilibrios contrarios.

But I want neither substance nor shadow, divinest of voices,
I require but my freedom, my passion's humanity
in that darkest corner of wind unwanted by others.
My passion's humanity!

The water-dogs pace one another
and the wind lies in wait for the negligent tree trunk.
O immemorial voice! scorch with your tongue
these voices of talcum and tinsel!

Let me blubber, since now I am minded to,
like the child left to wail on a seat in the rear.
Am neither all poet, all man, or all leaf,
but only the pulse of a wound that probes to the opposite side.

Let me blubber and blurt out my name—
rose, hemlock, or child—on the lake-shore,
speaking the blood-truths of men, and uprooting
whatever is left of the sneer and suggestion of words.

Not so much! Not so much! mine never to question, but seek
the voice that will lap at my fingertips, freed.
In the maze of the screens my nakedness bends to retrieve
the moon's castigation and the clock that is covered with ashes.

Or that way I spoke.
That way I spoke while Saturn delayed all the trains
and fog and illusion and death were hunting me down.
And hunted me down,
where the cows with an equerry's forefoot sometime were heard,
and my body, in the poise of the counterweights, floated.

CIELO VIVO

Yo no podré quejarme
si no encontré lo que buscaba.
Cerca de las piedras sin jugo y los insectos vacíos
no veré el duelo del sol con las criaturas en carne viva.

Pero me iré al primer paisaje
de choques, líquidos y rumores
que trasmina a niño recién nacido
y donde toda superficie es evitada,
para entender que lo que busco tendrá su blanco de alegría
cuando yo vuelo mezclado con el amor y las arenas.

Allí no llega la escarcha de los ojos apagados
ni el mugido del árbol asesinado por la oruga.
Allí todas las formas guardan entrelazadas
una sola expresión frenética de avance.

No puedes avanzar por los enjambres de corolas
porque el aire disuelve tus dientes de azúcar,
ni puedes acariciar la fugaz hoja del helecho
sin sentir el asombro definitivo del marfil.

Allí bajo las raíces y en la médula del aire
se comprende la verdad de las cosas equivocadas,
el nadador de níquel que acecha la onda más fina
y el rebaño de vacas nocturnas con rojas patitas de mujer.

Yo no podré quejarme
si no encontré lo que buscaba;
pero me iré al primer paisaje de humedades y latidos
para entender que lo que busco tendrá su blanco de alegría
cuando yo vuelo mezclado con el amor y las arenas.

HEAVEN ALIVE

I cannot complain
if all that I wanted eludes me.
In the sapless world of the stone and the void of the insect
I shall not envision a duel of sun with the creatures of festering
    flesh.

I go into genesis' landscape
of rumblings, collisions, and waters
that drench all the newly-born,
and shun all the surfaces,
to understand rightly my target-convergence in joy
when passion is mingled with dust and I rise upon air.

There the eye's dissolution cannot enter, like frost,
nor the bleating of shade-trees laid waste by the worm.
The genius of form weaves the web of a single relation:
passion's unaltering gaze toward the still-to-be-born.

See, you cannot advance through the swarm of corollas
lest a current of air melt the sweets of your teeth,
or touch with your love the fugitive frond of the fern
in your consummate terror of ivory.

Under roots, in the pith of the air, there
the truth of all dubious circumstance closes.
The swimmer of nickel is trapped in the filmiest ripple
with the flocks of the night-grazing cows, rosy-footed, like girls.

I cannot complain
if all that I wanted eludes me;
I go into genesis' landscape of dews and pulsations
to understand rightly my target-convergence in joy
when passion is mingled with dust and I rise upon air.

Vuelo fresco de siempre sobre lechos vacíos,
sobre grupos de brisas y barcos encallados.
Tropiezo vacilante por la dura eternidad fija
y amor al fin sin alba. Amor. ¡Amor visible¡

Eden Mills, Vermont, 24 de agosto de 1929

Fresh elevations forever, on the river-bed's hollow,
over volleys of wind and boats banked in the shallows,
where, uncertain, through stopped and unyielding eternity—
through love without sunrise—I reel to the end. O visible love!

Eden Mills, Vermont, August 24, 1929

V *EN LA CABAÑA DEL FARMER*

(Campo de Newburg)

A Concha Méndez y Manuel Altolaguirre

EL NIÑO STANTON

—*Do you like me?*
—*Yes, and you?*
—*Yes, yes.*

Cuando me quedo solo
me quedan todavía tus diez años,
los tres caballos ciegos,
tus quince rostros con el rostro de la pedrada
y las fiebres pequeñas heladas sobre las hojas del maíz.
Stanton, hijo mío, Stanton.
A las doce de la noche el cáncer salía por los pasillos
y hablaba con los caracoles vacíos de los documentos,
el vivísimo cáncer lleno de nubes y termómetros
con su casto afán de manzana para que lo piquen los ruiseñores.
En la casa donde no hay un cáncer
se quiebran las blancas paredes en el delirio de la astronomía
y por los establos más pequeños y en las cruces de los bosques
brilla por muchos años el fulgor de la quemadura.
Mi dolor sangraba por las tardes
cuando tus ojos eran dos muros,
cuando tus manos eran dos países
y mi cuerpo rumor de hierba.
Mi agonía buscaba su traje,
polvorienta, mordida por los perros,
y tú la acompañaste sin temblar
hasta la puerta del agua oscura.
¡Oh mi Stanton, idiota y bello entre los pequeños animalitos,
con tu madre fracturada por los herreros de las aldeas,
con un hermano bajo los arcos,
otro comido por los hormigueros,

V *IN THE FARMER'S CABIN*

(COUNTRY NEAR NEWBURG)

For Concha Méndez and Manuel Altolaguirre

LITTLE BOY STANTON

Do you like me?
Yes, and you?
Yes, yes.

Alone in myself,
your ten years stay with me still,
the three blind horses,
your fifteen likenesses, each with the look like the hurt of a stone
and the diminutive fevers iced on the blades of the corn.
O Stanton, Stanton, my son!
At midnight the cancer went forth in the passage-ways,
and talked with the husks of the dead depositions,
most savage of cancers, full of clouds and thermometers
with its virgin concern for an apple the nightingale pierces.
In the house where the cancer is not,
the white walls are cracked in a rage of astronomy
and through the littlest mangers of all and the forks of the forests
year after year glows the blaze of the smut.
Each noon my pang bled afresh
when your eyes were two barriers,
when your hands were two countries
and my body a whimper of grass.
My agony sought its investiture,
gritty and cur-bitten
and you went by her side, without qualm,
to the door of dark water.
O Stanton, comely and daft in the creaturely world of the little,
with your mother broken by smiths in the village,
and one brother under the archways
and another devoured on the ant heaps,

73

y el cáncer sin alambradas latiendo por las habitaciones!
Hay nodrizas que dan a los niños
ríos de musgo y amargura de pie
y algunas negras suben a los pisos para repartir filtro de rata.
Porque es verdad que la gente
quiere echar las palomas a las alcantarillas
y yo sé lo que esperan los que por la calle
nos oprimen de pronto las yemas de los dedos.

Tu ignorancia es un monte de leones, Stanton.
El día que el cáncer te dió una paliza
y te escupió en el dormitorio donde murieron los huéspedes en la
      epidemia
y abrió su quebrada rosa de vidrios secos y manos blandas
para salpicar de lodo las pupilas de los que navegan,
tú buscaste en la hierba mi agonía,
mi agonía con flores de terror,
mientras que el agrio cáncer mudo que quiere acostarse contigo
pulverizaba rojos paisajes por las sábanas de amargura,
y ponía sobre los ataúdes
helados arbolitos de ácido bórico.
Stanton, véte al bosque con tus arpas judías,
véte para aprender celestiales palabras
que duermen en los troncos, en nubes, en tortugas,
en los perros dormidos, en el plomo, en el viento,
en lirios que no duermen, en aguas que no copian,
para que aprendas, hijo, lo que tu pueblo olvida.

Cuando empiece el tumulto de la guerra
dejaré un pedazo de queso para tu perro en la oficina.
Tus diez años serán las hojas
que vuelan en los trajes de los muertos,
diez rosas de azufre débil
en el hombro de mi madrugada.
Y yo, Stanton, yo solo, en olvido,
con tus caras marchitas sobre mi boca,
iré penetrando a voces las verdes estatuas de la Malaria.

and the cancer, unquarantined, baying the houses!
There are nursemaids who give up to children
rivers of seaweed, and the gall of the vertical posture,
negresses mounting the stairs to divide up the rat-potion.
For certain it is there are those
who want to cast doves into sewers
and I know the intent of those others
who nudge us with fingertips, suddenly, out in the streets.

Your mindlessness, Stanton, is a mountain of lions.
The day that the cancer bludgeoned you down
and spat on you, in the beds where the guests of contagion lay
    dying,
it splintered a rose of parched glass and solicitous fingers opened
to muddy the mariners' eye,
and you sought in the grass for my agony,
my agony whose blossom was terror,
while, mute and acerb, the cancer longed to lie down with you,
in the crush of red landscapes under the bitter bedsheet,
and fixed on the coffinlids,
its saplings of glazed boric acid.
Stanton, go to the groves with your jew's-harp,
go study the heavenly words
that slumber in tree trunks, in clouds, in tortoises,
in the snore of the dog, in lead, in the wind,
in lilies that never take rest, in unmimicking water:
Learn, little son, what your kin has forgotten.

When the rout of the fighting breaks in
I'll leave morsels of cheese for your dog in the office.
Your ten years will be leaves
to whirl on the cloths of the dead,
ten roses of languishing sulphur
on my sunrise's shoulder.
It is I, Stanton, I alone, in forgetfulness,
with your faces that fade on my mouth:
I enter the statue's malarial green, with a cry, and move on.

VACA

A Luis Lacasa

Se tendió la vaca herida.
Árboles y arroyos trepaban por sus cuernos.
Su hocico sangraba en el cielo.

Su hocico de abejas
bajo el bigote lento de la baba.
Un alarido blanco puso en pie la mañana.

Las vacas muertas y las vivas,
rubor de luz o miel de establo,
balaban con los ojos entornados.

Que se enteren las raíces
y aquel niño que afila su navaja
de que ya se pueden comer la vaca.

Arriba palidecen
luces y yugulares.
Cuatro pezuñas tiemblan en el aire.

Que se entere la luna
y esa noche de rocas amarillas:
que ya se fué la vaca de ceniza.

Que ya se fué balando
por el derribo de los cielos yertos
donde meriendan muerte los borrachos.

COW

For Luis Lacasa

The hurt cow, outstretched.
Freshet and forest borne up on her horns.
Her muzzle bled in the sky.

Her muzzle, a bee-swarm
under the gradual mustache of saliva.
A white ululation alerted the morning.

The cows, the quick and the dead,
the ripening light or the honey of stables,
bawling with half-opened eyes.

Let the root be advised,
and the boy who whets down the knife-edge:
they can feed on the fat of the cow.

The lights and the jugulars
pale overhead.
Four shuddering hooves in the air.

Let the moon be advised
and night's yellowing stone:
the cow has moved off in an ember.

Moved off and goes bawling
through the wastes of stark sky
where the drunkards nibble on death.

NIÑA AHOGADA EN EL POZO

(GRANADA Y NEWBURG)

Las estatuas sufren por los ojos con la oscuridad de los ataúdes,
pero sufren mucho más por el agua que no desemboca.
Que no desemboca.

El pueblo corría por las almenas rompiendo las cañas de los
      pescadores.
¡Pronto! ¡Los bordes! ¡De prisa! Y croaban las estrellas tiernas.
. . . que no desemboca.

Tranquila en mi recuerdo, astro, círculo, meta,
lloras por las orillas de un ojo de caballo.
. . . que no desemboca.

Pero nadie en lo oscuro podrá darte distancias,
sin afilado límite, porvenir de diamante.
. . . que no desemboca.

Mientras la gente busca silencios de almohada
tú lates para siempre definida en tu anillo.
. . . que no desemboca.

Eterna en los finales de unas ondas que aceptan
combate de raíces y soledad prevista.
. . . . que no desemboca.

¡Ya vienen por las rampas! ¡Levántate del agua!
¡Cada punto de luz te dará una cadena!
. . . que no desemboca.

Pero el pozo te alarga manecitas de musgo,
insospechada ondina de su casta ignorancia.
. . . que no desemboca.

No, que no desemboca. Agua fija en un punto,
respirando con todos sus violines sin cuerdas
en la escala de las heridas y los edificios deshabitados.
      ¡Agua que no desemboca!

LITTLE GIRL DROWNED IN THE WELL

(GRANADA AND NEWBURG)

The eyes of the statues convulse on the coffin's obscurity,
but the water that never disgorges is a harder affliction.
Never disgorges.

The town fled to the battlements, breaking the fishermen's poles.
Quick! Hurry! The ledges! And starlight was croaking like frogs.
. . . that never disgorges.

Calm in my afterthought, star, zenith, corona,
you weep on the shores that encircle the eye of a horse.
. . . that never disgorges.

In the darkness, there is no one to give you the distances,
nor blade of the bounding-line, or future of diamond.
. . . that never disgorges.

While others seek for the stillness of pillows
your pulse-beat goes on in your finger-ring's margin, eternally.
. . . that never disgorges.

In the billow's conclusion, eternally, granting
isolation foreknown and the war of the roots.
. . that never disgorges.

They come to the breakwater! Step up from the water!
Each scintillation awaits you, like links in a chain!
. . . that never disgorges.

But the well reaches out little fingers of lichen,
inconceivable nymph of your candid delusion.
. . . that never disgorges.

No, never disgorges. O water fixed to a point,
rising and falling with your violins stripped of their strings
on the scale of a wound and the void of the derelict dwellings.
Water that never disgorges.

VI   *INTRODUCCION A LA MUERTE*

(POEMAS DE LA SOLEDAD EN VERMONT)

Para Rafael Sánchez Ventura

MUERTE

Para Isidoro de Blas

¡Qué esfuerzo!
¡Qué esfuerzo del caballo por ser perro!
¡Qué esfuerzo del perro por ser golondrina!
¡Qué esfuerzo de la golondrina por ser abeja!
¡Qué esfuerzo de la abeja por ser caballo!
Y el caballo,
¡qué flecha aguda exprime de la rosa!
¡qué rosa gris levanta de su belfo!
Y la rosa,
¡qué rebaño de luces y alaridos
ata en el vivo azúcar de su tronco!
Y el azúcar,
¡qué puñalitos sueña en su vigilia!
Y los puñales diminutos,
¡qué luna sin establos!, ¡qué desnudos,
piel eterna y rubor, andan buscando!
Y yo, por los aleros,
¡qué serafín de llamas busco y soy!
Pero el arco de yeso,
¡qué grande, que invisible, qué diminuto,
sin esfuerzo!

VI _INTRODUCTION TO DEATH_

(POEMS OF SOLITUDE IN VERMONT)

For Rafael Sánchez Ventura

DEATH

For Isidoro de Blas

The strain of it!
Horse would be dog,
dog would be swallow,
swallow, a wasp,
wasp would be horse!
And the horse—
how deadly an arrow it wrings from the rose!
how wanly the rose rises out of his underlip!
And the rose—
what a concourse of lights and alarms
bound in the hurrying sweets of its stem!
And the sugar—
what little stilettoes it dreams in its vigils!
And the little stilettoes—
what mangerless moons they seek out! what nudes
of flushed, indestructible flesh!
And I, on the eaves,
who strain to be fiery seraph, and am—
while the plaster pendentive,
so invisible, vast, and so small—
strains not at all!

NOCTURNO DEL HUECO

I

Para ver que todo se ha ido,
para ver los huecos y los vestidos,
¡dáme tu guante de luna,
tu otro guante perdido en la hierba,
amor mío!

Puede el aire arrancar los caracoles
muertos sobre el pulmón del elefante
y soplar los gusanos ateridos
de las yemas de luz o las manzanas.

Los rostros bogan impasibles
bajo el diminuto griterío de las yerbas
y en el rincón está el pechito de la rana
turbio de corazón y mandolina.

En la gran plaza desierta
mugía la bovina cabeza recién cortada
y eran duro cristal definitivo
las formas que buscaban el giro de la sierpe.

Para ver que todo se ha ido
dáme tu mudo hueco, ¡amor mío!
Nostalgia de academia y cielo triste.
¡Para ver que todo se ha ido!

Dentro de ti, amor mío; por tu carne,
¡qué silencio de trenes bocarriba!
¡cuánto brazo de momia florecido!
¡qué cielo sin salida, amor, qué cielo!

Es la piedra en el agua y es la voz en la brisa
bordes de amor que escapan de su tronco sangrante.
Basta tocar el pulso de nuestro amor presente
para que broten flores sobre los otros niños.

NOCTURNE OF THE VOID

I

To see how all passes,
the void and the vesture together,
give me your gauntlet of moonlight,
and that other glove, lost in the grass,
O my love!

A stir in the air can pluck out the snail
dead in the elephant's lung,
and puff up the frost-stiffened worm
in the calyx of apples and light.

The indifferent faces float off
in the failing clamor of grass
and from the toad's little breast, in the corners,
a chaos of heart-beat and mandolins.

In the great, empty square
the head of a cow bawled, after the slaughterer,
and shapes sought the rounds of the serpent,
fixed in definitive crystal.

To see how all passes,
give me the hush of your emptiness, love!
the school-man's nostalgia and the woebegone sky.
To see how all passes!

In you, in your flesh, O my love,
what a silence of overturned trains!
How the mummified hand goes to flower!
What heaven, what passageless heaven, my love!

Stone among waters, voice on the wind,
Love's verge taking flight from its blood-spattered center.
Enough to set hands on the pulse of our manifest love
for the blossoms to break overhead for love's other children.

Para ver que todo se ha ido.
Para ver los huecos de nubes y ríos.
Dáme tus manos de laurel, amor.
¡Para ver que todo se ha ido!

Ruedan los huecos puros, por mí, por ti, en el alba
conservando las huellas de las ramas de sangre
y algún perfil de yeso tranquilo que dibuja
instantáneo dolor de luna apuntillada.

Mira formas concretas que buscan su vacío.
Perros equivocados y manzanas mordidas.
Mira el ansia, la angustia de un triste mundo fósil
que no encuentra el acento de su primer sollozo.

Cuando busco en la cama los rumores del hilo
has venido, amor mío, a cubrir mi tejado.
El hueco de una hormiga puede llenar el aire,
pero tú vas gimiendo sin norte por mis ojos.

No, por mis ojos no, que ahora me enseñas
cuatro ríos ceñidos en tu brazo,
en la dura barraca donde la luna prisionera
devora a un marinero delante de los niños.

Para ver que todo se ha ido
¡amor inexpugnable, amor huído!
No, no me des tu hueco,
¡que ya va por el aire el mío!
¡Ay de ti, ay de mí, de la brisa!
Para ver que todo se ha ido.

II

Yo.
Con el hueco blanquísimo de un caballo,
crines de ceniza. Plaza pura y doblada.

Yo.
Mi hueco traspasado con las axilas rotas.
Piel seca de uva neutra y amianto de madrugada.

To see how all passes.
The voids of the cloud and the river together.
Give me your laurel-leaf fingers, O love!
To see how all passes!

Out of me, out of you, the pure voids revolve in the dawn
keeping the imprint of blood in the branches,
some profile untroubled in chalk, that defines
the immediate woe of the dagger-struck moon.

See how the shapes of concretion seek out their vacancy.
The dog on a false scent, the bite in the apple.
Mark but the strain, the anxious, sad bone of the world
that nowhere encounters its note of primordial cry.

When I follow the murmuring threads to my bed
you are there to draw me to cover, my love.
The void of an ant is sufficient to overflow space,
yet here in my presence you lament without knowing the end.

Yet not in my presence; for now you uncover
four rivers of ash on your arm,
in the comfortless hutch where the criminal moon
devours the sailor while the children look on.

To see how all passes!
O intractable, runaway love!
Do not leave me your emptiness,
but suffer my own to be lost in the air!
And pity us—you and myself and the wind!
To see how all passes!

II

.

With that whitest void of a horse,
the ash of his mane. The immaculate square doubled back.

.

My void countercrossed by the sundering arm-pit.
The dried, neuter grape-skin and asbestos of dawn.

85

Toda la luz del mundo cabe dentro de un ojo.
Canta el gallo y su canto dura más que sus alas.

Yo.
Con el hueco blanquísimo de un caballo.
Rodeado de espectadores que tienen hormigas en las palabras.

En el circo del frío sin perfil mutilado.
Por los capiteles rotos de las mejillas desangradas.

Yo.
Mi hueco sin ti, ciudad, sin tus muertos que comen.
Ecuestre por mi vida definitivamente anclada.

Yo.
No hay siglo nuevo ni luz reciente.
Sólo un caballo azul y una madrugada.

The light of the world passes into the round of an eye.
The cock calls, and his cry will outdistance his wings.

I.

With that whitest void of a horse.
Circled by onlookers whose words swarm with ants.

In the circus of cold, undefined and disfigured.
Among splintering capitals, cheeks bled of color.

I.

My void always lacking you, city, your dead men at dinner.
Equestrian, unalterably lashed to my life.

I.

And no replenishing century or renewal of light.
Only the blue of a horse and a dawn.

PAISAJE CON DOS TUMBAS Y UN PERRO ASIRIO

Amigo,
levántate para que oigas aullar
al perro asirio.
Las tres ninfas del cáncer han estado bailando,
hijo mío.
Trajeron unas montañas de lacre rojo
y unas sábanas duras donde estaba el cáncer dormido.
El caballo tenía un ojo en el cuello
y la luna estaba en un cielo tan frío
que tuvo que desgarrarse su monte de Venus
y ahogar en sangre y ceniza los cementerios antiguos.

Amigo,
despierta, que los montes todavía no respiran
y las hierbas de mi corazón están en otro sitio.
No importa que estés lleno de agua de mar.
Yo amé mucho tiempo a un niño
que tenía una plumilla en la lengua
y vivimos cien años dentro de un cuchillo.
Despierta. Calla. Escucha. Incorpórate un poco.
El aullido
es una larga lengua morada que deja
hormigas de espanto y licor delirios.
Ya viene hacia la roca. ¡No alargues tus raíces!
Se acerca. Gime. No solloces en sueños, amigo.

¡Amigo!
Levántate para que oigas aullar
al perro asirio.

LANDSCAPE WITH TWO GRAVES AND
AN ASSYRIAN DOG

Friend,
rouse yourself, listen;
the Assyrian dog howls.
Cancer's three nymphs have been dancing,
my son.
Red mountains of lacquer they bore
and coarse sheets where the cancer was sleeping.
The horse with an eye in its neck
and the moon in its heaven so cold
she mangled the mound of her sex
and drowned the old graveyards in ashes and blood.

Friend,
wake up; even now the hills do not breathe
and the grass of my heart has moved on to another location.
What if you brim over with sea-water?
For a long time I cherished a child
with a feather's down on his tongue
and inside a knife we lived for a hundred years.
Wake and be quiet. Listen. Sit up a while.
The howling of dogs
is a great purple tongue that bestows
an ant's trepidation and a liquor of lilies.
It moves toward the rocks! Do not reach out your roots!
It nears. It whimpers. O friend, do not moan in your sleep.

Friend,
rouse yourself, listen:
the Assyrian dog howls.

RUINA

Sin encontrarse,
viajero por su propio torso blanco,
¡así iba el aire!

Pronto se vió que la luna
era una calavera de caballo
y el aire una manzana oscura.

Detrás de la ventana
con látigos y luces se sentía
la lucha de la arena con el agua.

Yo vi llegar las hierbas
y les eché un cordero que balaba
bajo sus dientecillos y lancetas.

Volaba dentro de una gota
la cáscara de pluma y celuloide
de la primer paloma.

Las nubes en manada
se quedaron dormidas contemplando
el duelo de las rocas con el alba.

Vienen las hierbas, hijo.
Ya suenan sus espadas de saliva
por el cielo vacío.

Mi mano, amor. ¡Las hierbas!
Por los cristales rotos de la casa
la sangre desató sus cabelleras.

Tú solo y yo quedamos.
Prepara tu esqueleto para el aire.
Yo solo y tú quedamos.

Prepara tu esqueleto.
Hay que buscar de prisa, amor, de prisa,
nuestro perfil sin sueño.

RUIN

Still unencountered,
wayfarer in his own white torso,
so went the wind.

Soon it was known that the moon
was a horse's skull
and the air a shadowy apple.

Behind shutters,
in whipthong and lustre, was waged
the contest of water and sand.

I saw that the grasses had come
and I cast forth a whimpering lamb
under their lancets and fangs.

There flew in a water-drop
in celluloid and feathers, the rind
of the dove of beginning.

Clouds in a flock
delayed in their slumber to ponder
the duel of the rock and the dawn.

The grasses have come. Child,
the spittle blades chime
under hollow heaven.

The grasses! Love, take my hand.
In a house's smashed windows
blood lets its long hair.

I and your sole self remain.
Prepare your skeleton for air.
You remain and my sole self.

Make ready your skeleton.
Love, hasten, there is left us to hasten
the dreamless quest of our profile.

LUNA Y PANORAMA DE LOS INSECTOS

(POEMA DE AMOR)

> *La luna en el mar riela,*
> *en la lona gime el viento*
> *y alza en blando movimiento*
> *olas de plata y azul.*
>
> —ESPRONCEDA

Mi corazón tendría la forma de un zapato
si cada aldea tuviera una sirena.
Pero la noche es interminable cuando se apoya en las enfermos
y hay barcos que buscan ser mirados para poder hundirse tranquilos.

Si el aire sopla blandamente
mi corazón tiene la forma de una niña.
Si el aire se niega a salir de los cañaverales
mi corazón tiene la forma de una milenaria boñiga de toro.

Bogar, bogar, bogar, bogar,
hacia el batallón de puntas desiguales,
hacia un paisaje de acechos pulverizados.
Noche igual de la nieve, de los sistemas suspendidos.
Y la luna.

¡La luna!
Pero no la luna.
La raposa de las tabernas,
el gallo japonés que se comió los ojos,
las hierbas masticadas.

No nos salvan las solitarias en los vidrios,
ni los herbolarios donde el metafísico
encuentra las otras vertientes del cielo.
Son mentira las formas. Sólo existe
el círculo de bocas del oxígeno.

MOON AND INSECT PANORAMA

(LOVE POEM)

> *The moon glows on the sea,*
> *the wind whines in the sail*
> *and raises a mild agitation*
> *of blue waves and silver.*
> —ESPRONCEDA

My heart would be shoe-shaped
if sirens lived in the villages.
But nighttime, that leans on the ailing, is endless
and the ships ask a witness of onlookers to sink to their peace.

In a temperate wind
my heart takes the form of a girl.
If the wind will not stir from the canebrakes
my heart takes the form of millennial cow-dung.

Stroke oar and stroke oar and stroke oar,
toward the battalion's irregular lance-points
and a country of pulverized ambush.
The level night of the snow, and the systems suspended aloft.
And the moon.

Ah, the moon!
Yet never the moon.
The fox in the barroom,
the Japanese gamecock that eats out its eyes,
the tooth-bitten grasses.

The tapeworm preserved under glass cannot save us,
nor the herbalist's lore where the metaphysician
confronts all the gradients of heaven.
The forms are a lie. Nothing exists
but the circle of oxygen mouths.

Y la luna.
Pero no la luna.
Los insectos,
los muertos diminutos por las riberas,
dolor en longitud,
yodo en un punto,
las muchedumbres en el alfiler,
el desnudo que amasa la sangre de todos,
y mi amor que no es un caballo ni una quemadura,
criatura de pecho devorado.
¡Mi amor!

Ya cantan, gritan, gimen: Rostro, ¡Tu rostro! Rostro.
Las manzanas son unas,
las dalias son idénticas,
la luz tiene un sabor de metal acabado
y el campo de todo un lustro cabrá en la mejilla de la moneda.
Pero tu rostro cubre los cielos del banquete.
¡Ya cantan!, ¡gritan!, ¡gimen!,
¡cubren!, ¡trepan!, ¡espantan!

Es necesario caminar, ¡de prisa!, por las ondas, por las ramas,
por las calles deshabitadas de la edad media que bajan al río,
por las tiendas de las pieles donde suena un cuerno de vaca herida,
por las escalas, ¡sin miedo!, por las escalas.
Hay un hombre descolorido que se está bañando en el mar;
es tan tierno que los reflectores le comieron jugando el corazón.
Y en el Perú viven mil mujeres, ¡oh insectos!, que noche y día
hacen nocturnos y desfiles entrecruzando sus propias venas.

Un diminuto guante corrosivo me detiene, ¡Basta!
En mi pañuelo he sentido el tris
de la primera vena que se rompe.
Cuida tus pies, amor mío, ¡tus manos!,

And the moon.
Yet never the moon.
The insects,
the inanimate mites on the shore,
woe's longitude,
the iodine mote,
the hordes on the point of a pin,
the naked one kneading our blood,
and my love, neither stallion nor firebrand,
the creature whose breast was despoiled.
O my love!

Now they sing; they whimper and shriek: That face! that face!
*   Ah, your face!*
The apples are equal,
the dahlias, identical,
the light has a taste of worn metal
and the field of a lustrum will cover the face of a coin.
But your face masks a banquet of heaven.
They sing! And they whimper! They shriek,
Mask, mount, and astonish!

Be quick! You must pass through the waves and the branches,
through the medieval, dead streets that go down to the river,
past the dealers in leather where the horn of the hurt cow is
      sounded,
up the stairway, unterrified, upward.
There a colorless man will swim out in the sea—
so fragile the play of the searchlights have eaten his heart.
And a thousand women live on in Peru. Insects! who day and
      night
weave columns and night-marches countercrossed on their veins.

A small glove's corrosive detains me. Enough!
I felt on my handkerchief the crash
of the first vein breaking open like glass.
Look to your feet, oh my darling! And your hands!

95

ya que yo tengo que entregar mi rostro,
mi rostro!, mi rostro!, ¡ay, mi comido rostro!

Este fuego casto para mi deseo,
esta confusión por anhelo de equilibrio,
este inocente dolor de pólvora en mis ojos,
aliviará la angustia de otro corazón
devorado por las nebulosas.

No nos salva la gente de las zapaterías,
ni los paisajes que se hacen música al encontrar las llaves oxidadas.
Son mentira los aires. Sólo existe
una cunita en el desván
que recuerda todas las cosas.
Y la luna.
Pero no la luna.
Los insectos,
los insectos solos,
crepitantes, mordientes, estremecidos, agrupados,
y la luna
con un guante de humo sentada en la puerta de sus derribos.
¡¡La luna!!

Nueva York, 4 de enero de 1930

And now I must yield up my face,
my face! Oh, my face! My face wholly ravaged!

This pure fire for my longing,
this bedlam in wished-for equilibrium,
this innocent, gunpowder pang in my eyes,
will temper another heart's anguish
devoured by the nebulae.

The shoemaker's kind will not save us,
nor the landscapes that sing in a rusty encounter of keys.
The tunes are a lie. Nothing exists
but the attic's small cradle
where all is remembered.
And the moon.
Yet never the moon.
The insects,
the insects alone,
the cracklers, the stingers, the tremblers, the swarmers,
and the moon
sunk in the door of its ruins, with a gauntlet of smoke.
Ah, the moon!

New York, January 4, 1930

VII VUELTA A LA CIUDAD

Para Antonio Hernández Soriano

NEW YORK
(OFICINA Y DENUNCIA)

Para Fernando Vela

Debajo de las multiplicaciones
hay una gota de sangre de pato.
Debajo de las divisiones
hay una gota de sangre de marinero.
Debajo de las sumas, un río de sangre tierna;
un río que viene cantando
por los dormitorios de los arrabales,
y es plata, cemento o brisa
en el alba mentida de New York.
Existen las montañas, lo sé.
Y los anteojos para la sabiduría,
lo sé. Pero yo no he venido a ver el cielo.
He venido para ver la turbia sangre,
la sangre·que lleva las máquinas a las cataratas
y el espíritu a la lengua de la cobra.
Todos los días se matan en New York
cuatro millones de patos,
cinco millones de cerdos,
dos mil palomas para el gusto de los agonizantes,
un millón de vacas,
un millón de corderos
y dos millones de gallos
que dejan los cielos hechos añicos.
Más vale sollozar afilando la navaja
o asesinar a los perros en las alucinantes cacerías
que resistir en la madrugada
los interminables trenes de leche,
los interminables trenes de sangre,
y los trenes de rosas maniatadas

VII RETURN TO THE CITY

For Antonio Hernández Soriano

NEW YORK
(OFFICE AND DENUNCIATION)

For Fernando Vela

Under the multiplications
is a drop of duck's blood.
Beneath the divisions,
the sailor's blood-drop.
Under the sums, a river of delicate blood;
a river flows singing
by suburb and dormitory;
is sea-breeze, silver, cement,
in the counterfeit dawn of New York.
The mountains exist; I know that.
And the oracle's eye-glasses;
I know it. But I have not come here to ogle the sky.
Am here to look upon blood, the silt
in the blood that delivers the engines over the waterfalls
and our souls to the fang of the cobra.
They butcher each day in New York
four million ducks,
five million hogs,
two thousand doves, to a dying man's pleasure;
one million cows,
one million lambs,
two million roosters
that splinter all heaven to rubble.
Better sob while we strop down the razor
or murder the dogs in the blaze of the chase,
than oppose in the dawn
the interminable milk trains,
the blood trains, interminable,
the trains of the manacled roses, chained

por los comerciantes de perfumes.
Los patos y las palomas
y los cerdos y los corderos
ponen sus gotas de sangre
debajo de las multiplicaciones;
y los terribles alaridos de las vacas estrujadas
llenan de dolor el valle
donde el Hudson se emborracha con aceite.
Yo denuncio a toda la gente
que ignora la otra mitad,
la mitad irredimible
que levanta sus montes de cemento
donde laten los corazones
de los animalitos que se olvidan
y donde caeremos todos
en la última fiesta de los taladros.
Os escupo en la cara.
La otra mitad me escucha
devorando, orinando, volando en su pureza
como los niños de las porterías
que llevan frágiles palitos
a los huecos donde se oxidan
las antenas de los insectos.
No es el infierno, es la calle.
No es la muerte, es la tienda de frutas.
Hay un mundo de ríos quebrados y distancias inasibles
en la patita de ese gato quebrada por el automóvil,
y yo oigo el canto de la lombriz
en el corazón de muchas niñas.
Óxido, fermento, tierra estremecida.
Tierra tú mismo que nadas por los números de la oficina.
¿Qué voy a hacer, ordenar los paisajes?
¿Ordenar los amores que luego son fotografías,
que luego son pedazos de madera y bocanadas de sangre?
No, no; yo denuncio,
yo denuncio la conjura
de estas desiertas oficinas

by the drummers of perfume.
The ducks and the doves,
and the hogs and the lambs
shed their blood-drops
under the multiplications;
and the terrible babel of cattle, stampeding,
fills all the valley with weeping
where the Hudson flows, drunk upon oil.
I accuse all the living
who have put out of mind all those others,
the unregenerate half
who pile up the mountains of asphalt
where the hearts
of the little, unmemoried creatures beat on;
and we all shall go down
in the ultimate feasts of the drill.
I spit in your face: see.
The other half hears me,
they who feed themselves, fly, and make water, undefiled,
like the gatekeeper's children
who carry the breakable straw
to the pot-holes where rust
all the insect antennae.
This is not hell, but a street.
Not death, but a fruit-stand.
Here is the world of the sundering rivers, the infinite distances
in a cat's paw smashed by the motorist.
I hear out the song of the worm
in the manifold heart of the children.
Rust, fermentation, earth tremors.
Earthen yourself, who float on the office's numerals.
What shall I do now? Align all the landscapes?
Muster the lovers who turn into photographs
and later are splinters of wood, and mouthfuls of blood?
No, never; I accuse!
I accuse the conspiracy
of untenable offices

101

que no radian las agonías,
que borran los programas de la selva,
y me ofrezco a ser comido por las vacas estrujadas
cuando sus gritos llenan el valle
donde el Hudson se emborracha con aceite.

whose agonies never ray forth;
that efface the design of the forest;
and I offer myself to be eaten by cattle, the rabble
whose outcries have filled all the valley
where the Hudson flows, drunk upon oil.

CEMENTERIO JUDÍO

Las alegres fiebres huyeron a las maromas de los barcos
y el judío empujó la verja con el pudor helado del interior de la
      lechuga.

Los niños de Cristo dormían
y el agua era una paloma
y la madera era una garza
y el plomo era un colibrí
y aun las vivas prisiones de fuego
estaban consoladas por el salto de la langosta.

Los niños de Cristo bogaban y los judíos llenaban los muros
con un solo corazón de paloma
por el que todos querían escapar.
Las niñas de Cristo cantaban y las judías miraban la muerte
con un solo ojo de faisán,
vidriado por la angustia de un millón de paisajes.

Los médicos ponen en el níquel sus tijeras y guantes de goma
cuando los cadáveres sienten en los pies
la terrible claridad de otra luna enterrada.
Pequeños dolores ilesos se acercan a los hospitales
y los muertos se van quitando un traje de sangre cada día.

Las arquitecturas de escarcha,
las liras y gemidos que se escapan de las hojas diminutas
en otoño, mojando las últimas vertientes,
se apagaban en el negro de los sombreros de copa.

La hierba celeste y sola de la que huye con miedo el rocío
y las blancas entradas de mármol que conducen al aire duro
mostraban su silencio roto por las huellas dormidas de los zapatos.

El judío empujó la verja;
pero el judío no era un puerto

JEWISH CEMETERY

Fevers of jubilee fled to the boat cables
and the Jew pressed the boat-rail with the frozen reserve in the
    lettuce's core.

Christ's little boy-children slept;
the sea was a pigeon,
the timber a heron,
the plummet a hummingbird,
and even the living asylums of fire
were consoled by the leap of the grasshopper.

Christ's boy-children rowed and the Jews thronged the walls
with the dove's single heart,
whose sign might deliver them all.
Christ's girl-children sang and the Jewesses looked upon death
with the single eye of a pheasant
glazed by the ache of a million perspectives.

The doctors laid out on the nickel their scissors and surgical
    gloves,
while the corpses felt on their feet
the terrible glare of another moon, buried beneath.
Little inviolate sorrows come within hospital range
and daily a garment of blood is put off by the dead.

The frost's architecture,
the lyres and laments that break from the tapering leaves,
drenching the furthermost hill-slopes in autumn,
guttered out in an opera hat's blackness.

The lonely, ineffable grass, the rout of the terrified dew,
the white vents of marble that give on unyielding air,
opened their stillness, disturbed by the slumbering shoe-print.

The Jew pressed the boat-rail;
but the Jew was no harbor

y las barcas de nieve se agolparon
por las escalerillas de su corazón:
las barcas de nieve que acechan
un hombre de agua que las ahogue,
las barcas de los cementerios
que a veces dejan ciegos a los visitantes.

Los niños de Cristo dormían
y el judío ocupó su litera.
Tres mil judíos lloraban en el espanto de las galerías
porque reunían entre todos con esfuerzo media paloma,
porque uno tenía la rueda de un reloj
y otro un botín con orugas parlantes
y otro una lluvia nocturna cargada de cadenas
y otro la uña de un ruiseñor que estaba vivo;
y porque la media paloma gemía
derramando una sangre que no era la suya.

Las alegres fiebres bailaban por las cúpulas humedecidas
y la luna copiaba en su mármol
nombres viejos y cintas ajadas.
Llegó la gente que come por detrás de las yertas columnas
y los asnos de blancos dientes
con los especialistas de las articulaciones.
Verdes girasoles temblaban
por los páramos del crepúsculo
y todo el cementerio era una queja
de bocas de cartón y trapo seco.
Ya los niños de Cristo se dormían
cuando el judío, apretando los ojos,
se cortó las manos en silencio
al escuchar los primeros gemidos.

Nueva York, 18 de enero de 1930

and the snow-boats were crowding
his heart's little ladders:
the snow-boats were waiting
a watery man who would drown them,
the ships of the graveyard
that sometimes have blinded the visitant.

Christ's boy-children slept,
and the Jew bedded down in his litter.
Three thousand Jews, in a terror of passage-ways, groaned;
for they strove to preserve half a pigeon between them;
and one had a watch-wheel,
and another a legging that swarmed with the talkative caterpillars,
and another a night-falling rain, clamped under chains,
and one a surviving nightingale's claw;
and they wept with the grieving one half of the pigeon
shedding blood-drops no longer its own.

Fevers of jubilee danced over dampening domes,
and the moon copied into her marble
old namesakes and tangles of ribbon.
There followed the others who eat behind motionless columns,
and the donkeys, white-toothed,
and the ligature experts.
Green sunflowers shook
on evening's cold uplands,
and the graveyard became like a groan
out of mouths of dry cardboard and dishrags;
Christ's boy-children dropped off to sleep
while the Jew, with a tightening eye,
lopped off his hands in the silence
as the first sounds of wailing were heard.

New York, January 18, 1930

CRUCIFIXIÓN

La luna pudo detenerse al fin por la curva blanquísima de los
    caballos.
Un rayo de luz violeta que se escapaba de la herida
proyectó en el cielo el instante de la circuncisión de un niño muerto.

La sangre bajaba por el monte y los ángeles la buscaban,
pero los cálices eran de viento y al fin llenaba los zapatos.
Cojos perros fumaban sus pipas y un olor de cuero caliente
ponía grises los labios redondos de los que vomitaban en las
    esquinas.
Y llegaban largos alaridos por el Sur de la noche seca.
Era que la luna quemaba con sus bujías el falo de los caballos.
Un sastre especialista en púrpura
había encerrado a las tres santas mujeres
y les enseñaba una calavera por los vidrios de la ventana.
Las tres en el arrabal rodeaban a un camello blanco
que lloraba porque al alba
tenía que pasar sin remedio por el ojo de una aguja.
¡Oh cruz! ¡Oh clavos! ¡Oh espina!
¡Oh espina clavada en el hueso hasta que se oxiden los planetas!
Como nadie volvía la cabeza, el cielo pudo desnudarse.
Entonces se oyó la gran voz y los fariseos dijeron:
Esa maldita vaca tiene las tetas llenas de leche.
La muchedumbre cerraba las puertas
y la lluvia bajaba por las calles decidida a mojar el corazón
mientras la tarde se puso turbia de latidos y leñadores
y la oscura ciudad agonizaba bajo el martillo de los carpinteros.

Esa maldita vaca
tiene las tetas llenas de perdigones,
dijeron los fariseos.
Pero la sangre mojó sus pies y los espíritus inmundos
estrellaban ampollas de laguna sobre las paredes del templo.
Se supo el momento preciso de la salvación de nuestra vida
porque la luna lavó con agua
las quemaduras de los caballos

CRUCIFIXION

The moon might rest, at last, on the whitest curve of a horse.
A beam of violet light that breaks from a wound
and blazons heaven with the dead child's instant of circumcision.

Blood fell on the mountains, and angels went in search of it,
but their chalices held only wind; blood spilled from their shoe-
    tops, at last.
Lame dogs puffed at their pipes, and the smell of hot leather
was gray on the circling lips of those who vomit on street-corners.
A clamor of weeping arose from the arid night of the South,
for the moon burned the phallus of horses in candle-fire.
Virtuoso of purple, a tailor
held three holy virgins at bay
and showed them a skull's shape through the glass of the window:
three, circling a camel
white, in the suburbs, and weeping, whose way
led through the needle's implacable eye in the dawn.
Crucifix, thorn-point, and nail!
Thorn nailed on the bone till galaxies rust in the sun!
With none to look back, the sky might uncover itself.
And a great voice spoke, and the pharisees said:
the milk is big in the dugs of the accursed cow.
A multitude bolted their doors
and the rain fell, resolute, drenching the heart, on the streets,
while evening clouded with woodcutters and barking dogs
and the darkened city died under the carpenter's hammer.

Surely the cow is accursed
with udders of bird-shot,
the pharisees said.
But their feet soaked up blood, and the wanton-in-heart
spattered the froth of the lake on the temple walls.
The infallible flash of our lifetime's redemption was revealed;
for the moon bathed the blistering horse-flesh
with water-drops—

y no la niña viva que callaron en la arena.
Entonces salieron los fríos cantando sus canciones
y las ranas encendieron sus lumbres en la doble orilla del río.
Esa maldita vaca, maldita, maldita, maldita
no nos dejará dormir, dijeron los fariseos,
y se alejaron a sus casas por el tumulto de la calle
dando empujones a los borrachos y escupiendo sal de los sacrificios
mientras la sangre los seguía con un balido de cordero.

Fué entonces
y la tierra despertó arrojando temblorosos ríos de polilla.

Nueva York, 18 de octubre de 1929

not the living shape of a child, but the carrion stilled on the sand.
And the frosts went abroad on the earth, singing songs,
and the frogs lit their flares on the double shore of the river.
The cow is accursed—is accursed, accursed—
that banishes sleep, said the pharisees,
and withdrew through the riotous streets to their houses,
jostling the drunkards and spitting the salt of the sacrifice,
while blood moved behind them, with a noise like the bleating of
    lambs.

So it befell, on a time;
and the whole earth awakened, shedding tremulous rivers of
    moths.

New York, October 18, 1929

VIII *DOS ODAS*

A mi editor Armando Guibert

GRITO HACIA ROMA
(Desde la torre de Crysler Building)

Manzanas levemente heridas
por finos espadines de plata,
nubes rasgadas por una mano de coral
que lleva en el dorso una almendra de fuego,
peces de arsénico como tiburones,
tiburones como gotas de llanto para cegar una multitud,
rosas que hieren
y agujas instaladas en los caños de la sangre,
mundos enemigos y amores cubiertos de gusanos
caerán sobre ti. Caerán sobre la gran cúpula
que untan de aceite las lenguas militares
donde un hombre se orina en una deslumbrante paloma
y escupe carbón machacado
rodeado de miles de campanillas.

Porque ya no hay quien reparta el pan ni el vino,
ni quien cultive hierbas en la boca del muerto,
ni quien abra los linos del reposo,
ni quien llore por las heridas de los elefantes.
No hay más que un millón de herreros
forjando cadenas para los niños que han de venir.
No hay más que un millón de carpinteros
que hacen ataúdes sin cruz.
No hay más que un gentío de lamentos
que se abren las ropas en espera de la bala.
El hombre que desprecia la paloma debía hablar,
debía gritar desnudo entre las columnas,
y ponerse una inyección para adquirir la lepra
y llorar un llanto tan terrible
que disolviera sus anillos y sus teléfonos de diamante.

TWO ODES
To My Publisher, Armando Guibert

CRY TO ROME
(From the Chrysler Building Tower)

Apples delicately bruised
by a supple blade's silver,
clouds broken by fistblows of coral
that carry a fiery cocoon on their backs,
the arsenical fish, like a shark,
the shark, like a tear-drop, blinding a multitude,
the rose, drawing blood,
and the needle-point finding the blood vessel,
the enemy worlds and the worm-eaten passions,
will cave in on you. They collapse on the sumptuous dome
that fattens the veteran's tongue with an oil-slick
where a man spills his urine on a dazzle of doves
and spits out a pulverized coal
as little bells circle by thousands.

For see: there is none to apportion the bread and the wine
or cultivate grass in the mouths of the dead,
none to turn back the linens of quiet
or weep for the elephant's wounds.
Only the blacksmiths,
a million, to temper the chains for the still-to-be-born.
Only carpenters,
a million, to hammer the coffins unmarked by a cross.
Only a rout of laments.
undoing their clothing and awaiting the bullet.
Whosoever despises the dove must declare himself,
must cry from the shafts in his nakedness,
must force in his bloodstream the leper's infection,
and shed the unspeakable tears
that melt down his rings and the telephone's diamond.

113

Pero el hombre vestido de blanco
ignora el misterio de la espiga,
ignora el gemido de la parturienta,
ignora que Cristo puede dar agua todavía,
ignora que la moneda quema el beso de prodigio
y da la sangre del cordero al pico idiota del faisán.

Los maestros enseñan a los niños
una luz maravillosa que viene del monte;
pero lo que llega es una reunión de cloacas
donde gritan las oscuras ninfas del cólera.
Los maestros señalan con devoción las enormes cúpulas sahumadas;
pero debajo de las estatuas no hay amor,
no hay amor bajo los ojos de cristal definitivo.
El amor está en las carnes desgarradas por la sed,
en la choza diminuta que lucha con la inundación;
el amor está en los fosos donde luchan las sierpes del hambre,
en el triste mar que mece los cadáveres de las gaviotas
y en el oscurísimo beso punzante debajo de las almohadas.
Pero el viejo de las manos traslúcidas
dirá: Amor, amor, amor,
aclamado por millones de moribundos;
dirá: amor, amor, amor,
entre el tisú estremecido de ternura;
dirá: paz, paz, paz,
entre el tirite de cuchillos y melones de dinamita;
dirá: amor, amor, amor,
hasta que se le pongan de plata los labios.

Mientras tanto, mientras tanto ¡ay! mientras tanto,
los negros que sacan las escupideras,
los muchachos que tiemblan bajo el terror pálido de los directores,
las mujeres ahogadas en aceites minerales,
la muchedumbre de martillo, de violín o de nube,
ha de gritar aunque le estrellen los sesos en el muro,
ha de gritar frente a las cúpulas,
ha de gritar loca de fuego,

But the white-suited man goes his way
with no thought of the corn-tassel's mystery,
with no thought of the birth-cry,
no thought of his Christ giving water eternally,
unmindful how money burns off the miraculous kiss,
shedding blood of the lamb on the idiot beak of the pheasant.

The masters reveal to the children
supernatural light moving out of the mountain;
but what has remained is a concourse of sewers
where the black nymphs of cholera cry.
In their ardor, they point the big cupolas out, fumed by the
        censers,
but under the images love has no place,
under the eyes of definitive crystal, love has no room.
Love waits in a thirst-broken flesh,
in the hovel that strives with the deluge,
in the ditch where the serpents of famine contend,
on a desolate ocean that dandles a carcass of gulls,
in the darkest kiss of them all, piercing under the bed-pillow.
But the old man, with light through his fingers,
will say: Love, love, love,
to the plaudits of perishing millions;
will say: love, love, love,
in the quivering tissue of tenderness;
will say: peace, peace, peace,
in the shudder of knives and the dynamite melons;
will say: love, love, love,
till his lips are sealed into silver.

Meanwhile, and meanwhile, and meanwhile:
the negro who sets out the cuspidors,
the terrorized boy shaking under the livid director,
women drowning in mineral oil,
the mob of the hammer, the fiddle, the cloud—
let them cry till they splinter their brains on a wall,
cry across cupolas,
fire-maddened,

ha de gritar loca de nieve,
ha de gritar con la cabeza llena de excremento,
ha de gritar como todas las noches juntas,
ha de gritar con voz tan desgarrada
hasta que las ciudades tiemblen como niñas
y rompan las prisiones del aceite y la música,
porque queremos el pan nuestro de cada día,
flor de aliso y perenne ternura desgranada,
porque queremos que se cumpla la voluntad de la Tierra
que da sus frutos para todos.

snow-maddened,
let them cry with a head full of excrement,
cry like all darkness made one,
cry with such ruinous voice
that the cities will tremble like girls
and break open the prisons of music and oil.
Give us that daily bread, for we wish it,
flower of the alder, threshed tenderness, world without end;
earth's will be done, for we wish it,
who offers her harvest to all.

ODA A WALT WHITMAN

Por el East River y el Bronx,
los muchachos cantaban enseñando sus cinturas,
con la rueda, el aceite, el cuero y el martillo.
Noventa mil mineros sacaban la plata de las rocas
y los niños dibujaban escaleras y perspectivas.

Pero ninguno se dormía,
ninguno quería ser el río,
ninguno amaba las hojas grandes,
ninguno la lengua azul de la playa.

Por el East River y el Queensborough
los muchachos luchaban con la industria,
y los judíos vendían al fauno del río
la rosa de la circuncisión
y el cielo desembocaba por los puentes y los tejados
manadas de bisontes empujadas por el viento.

Pero ninguno se detenía,
ninguno quería ser nube,
ninguno buscaba los helechos
ni la rueda amarilla del tamboril.

Cuando la luna salga
las poleas rodarán para turbar el cielo;
un límite de agujas cercará la memoria
y los ataúdes se llevarán a los que no trabajan.

Nueva York de cieno,
Nueva York de alambres y de muerte.
¿Qué ángel llevas oculto en la mejilla?
¿Qué voz perfecta dirá las verdades del trigo?
¿Quién el sueño terrible de tus anémonas manchadas?

Ni un solo momento, viejo hermoso Walt Whitman,
he dejado de ver tu barba llena de mariposas,
ni tus hombros de pana gastados por la luna,
ni tus muslos de Apolo virginal,

ODE TO WALT WHITMAN

Along East River and the Bronx
the young men were singing, baring their waists,
with the wheel and the leather, the hammer, the oil.
Ninety thousand miners whittled silver from the rocks
and the boys traced ladders and perspectives.

But nobody slept
or wished to be: river;
none loved the big leaves
or the beach's blue tongue.

Along East River and Queensborough,
the young men were grappling with Industry.
The Jews sold the faun of the river
circumcision's rosette;
and the sky, over bridges and rooftops
emptied its buffalo herds to the push of the wind.

But nobody dawdled,
or wished to be: cloud;
none looked for the fern
or the drum's yellow wheel.

At moon-rise,
the block and the tackle will veer and startle the sky;
a zenith of needles will circle all memory in
and the coffins move off with the jobless.

Ah, filthy New York,
New York of cables and death.
What angel do you carry, concealed in your cheek?
What ineffable voice will speak the truths of the wheat?
Who, the terrible dream of your tainted anemones?

Not for one moment, Walt Whitman, comely old man,
have I ceased to envision your beard full of butterflies,
your corduroy shoulders, worn thin by the moon,
your chaste, Apollonian thighs,

ni tu voz como una columna de ceniza;
anciano hermoso como la niebla
que gemías igual que un pájaro
con el sexo atravesado por una aguja,
enemigo del sátiro,
enemigo de la vid
y amante de los cuerpos bajo la burda tela.
Ni un solo momento, hermosura viril
que en montes de carbón, anuncios y ferrocarriles,
soñabas ser un río y dormir como un río
con aquel camarada que pondría en tu pecho
un pequeño dolor de ignorante leopardo.

Ni un solo momento, Adán de sangre, macho,
hombre solo en el mar, viejo hermoso Walt Whitman,
porque por las azoteas,
agrupados en los bares,
saliendo en racimos de las alcantarillas,
temblando entre las piernas de los chauffeurs
o girando en las plataformas de ajenjo,
los maricas, Walt Whitman, te señalan.

¡También ése! ¡También! Y se despeñan
sobre tu barba luminosa y casta,
rubios del norte, negros de la arena,
muchedumbres de gritos y ademanes,
como gatos y como las serpientes,
los maricas, Walt Whitman, los maricas
turbios de lágrimas, carne para fusta,
bota o mordisco de los domadores.

¡También ése! ¡También! Dedos teñidos
apuntan a la orilla de tu sueño
cuando el amigo come tu manzana
con un leve sabor de gasolina
y el sol canta por los ombligos
de los muchachos que juegan bajo los puentes.

your voice like a pillar of ashes;
patriarch, comely as mist,
you cried like a bird
whose sex is transfixed by a needle;
satyr's antagonist,
grapevine's antagonist,
and lover of bodies under the nap of the cloth.
Not for a moment, manly and comely one,
on mountains of railroads and coal and advertisements,
but you dreamed yourself river, and slept like a river,
with that comrade who took to your heart
the little complaint of the ignorant leopard.

Not a moment, blood-brother, Adam, and masculine,
lone man in a sea, Walt Whitman, comely old man—
for look!—on the rooftops,
or huddled in bars,
or leaping in packs from the gutters,
or held between legs of the motorist, shuddering,
or whirling on platforms of absinthe,
the perverts, Walt Whitman, all pointing you!

This one—and this one! They fall
on your decent and luminous beard,
the blonde-headed northerners, the blacks from the sand-dunes,
a legion of gestures and outcries,
catlike and serpentine—
perverts—the pack of them perverts, Walt Whitman—
grimy with tears, so much meat for the whiplash,
for the boot or the bite of the animal-tamers.

And this one! And this one! The taint of their fingernails point
to the brink of your dream
where the playfellow munches your apple
with a faint taste of gasoline,
and the sunlight sings out on the navels
of the boys at their games under bridges.

Pero tú no buscabas los ojos arañados,
ni el pantano oscurísimo donde sumergen a los niños,
ni la saliva helada,
ni las curvas heridas como panza de sapo
que llevan los maricas en coches y terrazas
mientras la luna los azota por las esquinas del terror.

Tú buscabas un desnudo que fuera como un río,
toro y sueño que junte la rueda con el alga,
padre de tu agonía, camelia de tu muerte,
y gimiera en las llamas de tu ecuador oculto.

Porque es justo que el hombre no busque su deleite
en la selva de sangre de la mañana próxima.
El cielo tiene playas donde evitar la vida
y hay cuerpos que no deben repetirse en la aurora.

Agonía, agonía, sueño, fermento y sueño.
Éste es el mundo, amigo, agonía, agonía.
Los muertos se descomponen bajo el reloj de las ciudades,
la guerra pasa llorando con un millón de ratas grises,
los ricos dan a sus queridas
pequeños moribundos iluminados,
y la vida no es noble, ni buena, ni sagrada.

Puede el hombre, si quiere, conducir su deseo
por vena de coral o celeste desnudo.
Mañana los amores serán rocas y el Tiempo
una brisa que viene dormida por las ramas.

Por eso no levanto mi voz, viejo Walt Whitman,
contra el niño que escribe
nombre de niña en su almohada,
ni contra el muchacho que se viste de novia
en la oscuridad del ropero,
ni contra los solitarios de los casinos
que beben con asco el agua de la prostitución,

But you never went looking for the scar on the eye,
or the overcast swamp where the boys are submerged,
or the freezing saliva
or the contours, split open, like the sac of the toad,
that the perverts in taxis and terraces carry
as the moon whips them on into terrified corners.

You looked for a nude that could be like a river,
the bull and the dream that could merge, like seaweed and wheel,
sire of your agony, your mortality's camellia,
to cry in the flames of your secret equator.

It is fitting that no man should seek
in another day's thickets of blood for his pleasure.
Heaven has shores for our flights out of life,
and the corpse need not make itself over at dawn.

Agony, agony, dream, ferment and dream.
It is the world's way, my friend: agony, agony.
Under the town-clock the dead decompose.
War takes its course with a million gray sewer-rats, sobbing.
The well-to-do will to their darlings
little candle-lit death-beds,
and life is not noble, or wholesome, or holy.

Yet we might, if we would, lead our appetite on
through the vein of the coral or the heaven-sent nude.
Tomorrow our passion is rock, and Time,
a wind come to sleep in the branches.

Wherefore my voice is not raised
to admonish the boy who inscribes
a girl's name on his pillow, Walt Whitman, old friend;
not to shame the young man who dresses himself like a bride
in the dark of the clothes-closet,
or the stags of the dance-hall
who drink at the waters of whoredom and sicken,

ni contra los hombres de mirada verde
que aman al hombre y queman sus labios en silencio.
Pero sí contra vosotros, maricas de las ciudades,
de carne tumefacta y pensamiento inmundo,
madres de lodo, arpías, enemigos sin sueño
del Amor que reparte coronas de alegría.

Contra vosotros siempre, que dais a los muchachos
gotas de sucia muerte con amargo veneno.
Contra vosotros siempre,
Faeries de Norteamérica,
Pájaros de la Habana,
Jotos de Méjico,
Sarasas de Cádiz,
Apios de Sevilla,
Cancos de Madrid,
Floras de Alicante,
Adelaidas de Portugal.

¡Maricas de todo el mundo, asesinos de palomas!
Esclavos de la mujer, perras de sus tocadores,
abiertos en las plazas con fiebre de abanico
o emboscadas en yertos paisajes de cicuta.

¡No haya cuartel! La muerte
mana de vuestros ojos
y agrupa flores grises en la orilla del cieno.
¡No haya cuartel! ¡Alerta!
Que los confundidos, los puros,
los clásicos, los señalados, los suplicantes
os cierren las puertas de la bacanal.

Y tú, bello Walt Whitman, duerme a orillas del Hudson
con la barba hacia el polo y las manos abiertas.
Arcilla blanda o nieve, tu lengua está llamando
camaradas que velen tu gacela sin cuerpo.
Duerme, no queda nada.

or the green apparition of men
who cherish mankind and burn out their lips in the silence.
But you! against all of you, perverts of the cities,
immodest of thought and tumescent of flesh,
mothers of filthiness, harpies, sleeplessly thwarting
the Love that apportions us garlands of pleasure.

Always against you, whosoever bestow upon boys
the foul drop of death with wormwood of venom.
Against you to the end!
North American *fairies,*
Pajaros of Havana,
Jotos of Mexico,
Sarasas of Cádiz,
Apios of Seville,
Cancos of Madrid,
Floras of Alicante,
Adelaidas of Portugal.

Perverts of the world, dove-killers!
Toadies of women, dressing-room bitches,
brazen in squares in a fever of fans
or ambushed in motionless landscapes of hemlock.

No quarter! Death
oozes out of your eyes
and clusters gray flowers at the edge of a bog.
No quarter! Beware!
Let the pure, the bewildered,
the illustrious, classic, and suppliant
shut the festival doors in your face.

And you, on the shores of the Hudson, handsome Walt Whitman,
    asleep
with your beard to the pole, open-handed.
In the delicate marl or the snow, your tongue always summoning
the comrades to watch your gazelle, disembodied in air.
Sleep on; for nothing abides.

Una danza de muros agita las praderas
y América se anega de máquinas y llanto.
Quiero que el aire fuerte de la noche más honda
quite flores y letras del arco donde duermes
y un niño negro anuncie a los blancos del oro
la llegada del reino de la espiga.

A dancing of walls rocks the meadows
and America drowns under engines and tears.
I could wish for a stirring of wind from the deepest abyss of the
    night
to undo all the letters and flowers from the arch where you drowse,
while a black boy declares to the gold-getting white
kingdom come in a tassel of corn.

IX *HUIDA DE NUEVA YORK*

(Dos Valses Hacia La Civilización)

PEQUEÑO VALS VIENÉS

En Viena hay diez muchachas,
un hombro donde solloza la muerte
y un bosque de palomas disecadas.
Hay un fragmento de la mañana
en el museo de la escarcha.
Hay un salón con mil ventanas.
¡Ay, ay, ay, ay!
Toma este vals con la boca cerrada.

Este vals, este vals, este vals,
de sí, de muerte y de coñac
que moja su cola en el mar.

Te quiero, te quiero, te quiero,
con la butaca y el libro muerto,
por el melancólico pasillo,
en el oscuro desván del lirio,
en nuestra cama de la luna
y en la danza que sueña la tortuga.
¡Ay, ay, ay, ay!
Toma este vals de quebrada cintura.

En Viena hay cuatro espejos
donde juegan tu boca y los ecos.
Hay una muerte para piano
que pinta de azul a los muchachos.
Hay mendigos por los tejados.
Hay frescas guirnaldas de llanto.
¡Ay, ay, ay, ay!
Toma este vals que se muere en mis brazos.

128

IX *FLIGHT FROM NEW YORK*

(TWO WALTZES TOWARD CIVILIZATION)

LITTLE VIENNESE WALTZ

Ten girls in Vienna
where death grieves on a shoulder,
and a forest of mummified pigeons.
A morsel of morning
in a showplace of frost.
A thousand panes in a hall.
Ay! Ay! Ay! Ay!
Take the waltz's time and be dumb.

This waltz and this waltz and this waltz,
whose impulse is brandy and death
that dampens its haunch in the sea.

And I love you, I love you, I love you,
with the corpse of a book and an overstuffed chair,
through the saddening aisle,
in a lily's black attic,
in our moon of a bed
and the dance that a turtle is dreaming.
Ay! Ay! Ay! Ay!
Take the broken-waist time of the waltz.

In Vienna are four looking-glasses
where your mouth and its echo carouses.
A pianoforte death
that blues the young men.
There are beggars on rooftops
and freshly-cut garlands of mourning.
Ay! Ay! Ay! Ay!
Take this waltz as it fails in my arms.

129

Porque te quiero, te quiero, amor mío,
en el desván donde juegan los niños,
soñando viejas luces de Hungría
por los rumores de la tarde tibia,
viendo ovejas y lirios de nieve
por el silencio oscuro de tu frente.
¡Ay, ay, ay, ay!
Toma este vals del "Te quiero siempre."

En Viena bailaré contigo
con un disfraz que tenga
cabeza de río.
¡Mira qué orillas tengo de jacintos!
Dejaré mi boca entre tus piernas,
mi alma en fotografías y azucenas,
y en las ondas oscuras de tu andar
quiero, amor mío, amor mío, dejar,
violín y sepulcro, las cintas del vals.

For: I love you, I love you, my darling,
in the attic where children pretend,
dreaming old lustres of Hungary
in the stir of the mild afternoon,
scanning the snow of the lamb and the lily
in the silence that shadows your forehead.
Ay! Ay! Ay! Ay!
Take the waltz's "I'll love you forever!"

We'll dance in Vienna
in a river's mouth
masked.
Only look at my hyacinth beaches!
My mouth I'll leave with your legs there, between,
and my soul in an album of snapshots and lilies,
and there in the darkening pulse of your motion
I'll yield up to my darling, my darling, my darling,
a ribband of waltz and the grave and the fiddle.

VALS EN LAS RAMAS

Cayó una hoja
y dos
y tres.
Por la luna nadaba un pez.
El agua duerme una hora
y el mar blanco duerme cien.
La dama
estaba muerte en la rama.
La monja
cantaba dentro de la toronja.
La niña
iba por el pino a la piña.
Y el pino
buscaba la plumilla del trino.
Pero el ruiseñor
lloraba sus heridas alrededor.
Y yo también
porque cayó una hoja
y dos
y tres.
Y una cabeza de cristal
y un violín de papel
y la nieve podría con el mundo
una a una
dos a dos
y tres a tres.
¡Oh, duro marfil de carnes invisibles!
¡Oh, golfo sin hormigas del amanecer!
Con el numen de las ramas,
con el ay de las damas,
con el cro de las ranas,
y el geo amarillo de la miel.
Llegará un torso de sombra
coronado de laurel.
Será el cielo para el viento

WALTZ IN THE BRANCHES

There fell a leaf
and two
and three.
And a fish swam into the moon.
The water slumbers an hour
and the white sea, a hundred.
A lady
lay dead in the branches. Still
the nun
in the grapefruit sang on.
The little girl
passed out of pine into cone.
And the pine
tried a feather-fine trill.
But the nightingale
wept in his circle of wounds,
as I
for the fall of a leaf
and two
and three.
A head of cut-crystal
and a fiddle of paper,
a world overcome by the snow,
by one and by one,
by two and by two,
by three and by three.
O ivory, hard in invisible flesh!
O void of the anthills of morning!

*　　*　　*　　*　　*　　*　　*
*　　*　　*　　*　　*　　*　　*
*　　*　　*　　*　　*　　*　　*
*　　*　　*　　*　　*　　*　　*

A torso of shadow will come
crowned with laurel.
The sky will stand firm to the wind

duro como una pared
y las ramas desgajadas
se irán bailando con él.
Una a una
alrededor de la luna,
dos a dos
alrededor del sol,
y tres a tres
para que los marfiles se duerman bien.

like a wall,
and the ruining branches
dance off.
One and by one
ringing the moon,
two and by two
ringing the sun,
three and by three and by three
till the ivories' slumber is sound.

---

* Four lines of untranslatable nonsense sounds have been omitted here.

X *EL POETA LLEGA A LA HABANA*

A Don Fernando Ortiz

SON DE NEGROS EN CUBA

Cuando llegue la luna llena iré a Santiago de Cuba,
iré a Santiago,
en un coche de agua negra.
Iré a Santiago.
Cantarán los techos de palmera.
Iré a Santiago.
Cuando la palma quiere ser cigüeña,
iré a Santiago.
Y cuando quiere ser medusa el plátano,
iré a Santiago.
Iré a Santiago,
con la rubia cabeza de Fonseca.
Iré a Santiago.
Y con la rosa de Romeo y Julieta
iré a Santiago.
¡Oh Cuba! ¡Oh ritmo de semillas secas!
Iré a Santiago.
¡Oh cintura caliente y gota de madera!
Iré a Santiago.
Arpa de troncos vivos. Caimán. Flor de tabaco.
Iré a Santiago.
Siempre he dicho que yo iría a Santiago
en un coche de agua negra.
Iré a Santiago.
Brisa y alcohol en las ruedas,
iré a Santiago.
Mi coral en la tiniebla,
iré a Santiago.
El mar ahogado en la arena,

X *THE POET ARRIVES IN HABANA*

For Don Fernando Ortiz

SON OF NEGROES IN CUBA

When a full moon rides over in Santiago de Cuba,
I'll go to Santiago
in a hack of black water.
I'll go to Santiago.
Palm-thatch will sing.
I'll go to Santiago.
When palm would be stork,
I'll go to Santiago.
When banana goes jellyfish
I'll go to Santiago.
I'll go to Santiago,
with the yellow-haired head of Fonseca.
I'll go to Santiago.
With the Romeo-Juliet rose
I'll go to Santiago.
O Cuba! Dry seeds in a cadence!
I'll go to Santiago.
Waist in a blaze, and a wood-drop!
I'll go to Santiago.
The living trunk, like a harp. Tobacco bloom. Crocodile.
I'll go to Santiago.
I have let it be known that I'll go to Santiago
in a hack of black water.
I'll go to Santiago.
Whiskey and wind in the wheels,
I'll go to Santiago.
My coral in darkness,
I'll go to Santiago,
sea strangled in sand,

iré a Santiago,
calor blanco, fruta muerta,
iré a Santiago.
¡Oh bovino frescor de cañaveras!
¡Oh Cuba! ¡Oh curva de suspiro y barro!
Iré a Santiago.

I'll go to Santiago,
white-heat, fruit-rot,
I'll go to Santiago.
O animal freshness of cane-fields!
Crescent of sea-silt and sighs. O Cuba!
I'll go to Santiago.

APPENDICES
AND
CRITICAL CHRONOLOGY

APPENDICES

I. TIERRA Y LUNA

Me quedo con el transparente hombrecillo
que come los huevos de la golondrina.
Me quedo con el niño desnudo
que pisotean los borrachos de Brooklyn
con las criaturas mudas que pasan bajo los arcos.
Con el arroyo de venas ansioso de abrir sus manecitas.

Tierra tan sólo. Tierra.
Tierra para los manteles estremecidos,
para la pupila viciosa de nube,
para las heridas recientes y el húmedo pensamiento.
Tierra para todo lo que huye de la tierra.

No es la ceniza en vilo de las cosas quemadas,
ni los muertos que mueven sus lenguas bajo los árboles.
Es la Tierra desnuda que bala por el cielo
y deja atrás los grupos ligeros de ballenas.

Es la tierra alegrísima, imperturbable nadadora,
la que yo encuentro en el niño y en las criaturas que pasan los arcos
Viva la tierra de mi pulso y del baile de los helechos
que deja a veces por el aire un duro perfil de Faraón.

Me quedo con la mujer fría
donde se queman los musgos inocentes;
me quedo con los borrachos de Brooklyn

APPENDICES

I. EARTH AND MOON

I stay with them always—the diaphanous
mannikin that feeds upon swallow's eggs.
The naked boy
trampled by drunkards in Brooklyn,
the creatures of silence passing under the arches.
The runnel of veins impatient to open its fingertips.

So lonely an earth. Earth.
Earth for the shuddering fall of the cloths,
for the dissolute pupil of cloud,
for the wound lately let and the moist meditation.
Earth for the exiled of earth taking flight from their element.

Not the cinder, aloft on the holocaust,
nor the tongues of the dead moving under the trees;
but Earth naked, Earth bleating its cry to the heavens
and leaving a delicate congress of whales in its wake.

Earth jubilant—imperturbable swimmer—
where we touch in the boy, in the creatures that pass by the
       arches.
Long live the earth of my pulses, of the dance in the ferns,
bestowing the contours of Pharaoh, unyielding, on air.

I stay with them: woman's frigidity
when the fires in the innocent mosses are kindled;
the drunkards of Brooklyn

143

que pisan al niño desnudo;
me quedo con los signos desgarrados
de la lenta comida de los osos.

Pero entonces bajo la luna despeñada por las escaleras
poniendo las ciudades de hule celeste y talco sensitivo
llenando de pies de mármol la llanura sin recodos
y olvidando, bajo las sillas, diminutas carcajadas de algodón.

¡Oh Diana, Diana, Diana vacía!
Convexa resonancia donde la abeja se vuelve loca.
Mi amor es paso, tránsito, larga muerte gustada,
nunca la piel ilesa de tu desnudo huído.

Es Tierra. ¡Dios mío! Tierra, lo que vengo buscando.
Embozo de horizonte, latido y sepultura.
Es dolor que se acaba y amor que se consume.
Torre de sangre abierta con las manos quemadas.

Pero la luna subía y bajaba las escaleras,
repartiendo lentejas desangradas en los ojos,
dando escobazos de plata a los niños de los muelles
y borrando mi apariencia por el término del aire.

Vermont, agosto 1929

trampling the nude underfoot: I stay with them.
I dwell with the agonized omens
of the gradual feast of the bear.

But under the moon, then, in its breakneck descent down the stair,
turning the cities to paradisaical oil-skin, to talcum,
crowding a point-blank perspective of plains with footfalls of
    marble
and forgetting the little guffaws of the cotton, under chairs.

Diana! Diana! Infertile Diana!
The bee has gone daft in your sounding convexity!
My love is displacement and passage, a long dying savored,
but never the flesh of your naked migrations, unscathed.

Heaven help me! It is Earth—it is Earth I pursue!
A folded horizon, a tremor, a grave.
It is anguish that comes to an end and passion that preys on itself.
A tower of blood in a hand's conflagration, laid bare.

Yet the moon will move upward and down on its stairway,
dividing the eye's bloody lentils,
dealing buffets of silver to the waifs on the wharves with its
    brooms,
and effacing my lone apparition on limits of air.

Vermont, August, 1929

II. PEQUEÑO POEMA INFINITO

Para Luis Cardoza y Aragón

Equivocar el camino
es llegar a la nieve
y llegar a la nieve
es pacer durante veinte siglos las hierbas de los cementerios.

Equivocar el camino
es llegar a la mujer,
la mujer que no teme la luz,
la mujer que mata dos gallos en un segundo,
la luz que no teme a los gallos
y los gallos que no saben cantar sobre la nieve.

Pero si la nieve se equivoca de corazón
puede llegar el viento Austro
y como el aire no hace caso de los gemidos
tendremos que pacer otra vez las hierbas de los cementerios.

Yo vi dos dolorosas espigas de cera
que enterraban un paisaje de volcanes
y vi dos niños locos que empujaban llorando las pupilas de un
      asesino.

Pero el dos no ha sido nunca un número
porque es una angustia y su sombra,
porque es la guitarra donde el amor se desespera,
porque es la demonstración de otro infinito que no es suyo
y es las murallas del muerto
y el castigo de la nueva resurrección sin finales.
Los muertos odian el número dos,
pero el número dos adormece a las mujeres
y como la mujer teme la luz
la luz tiembla delante de los gallos
y los gallos sólo saben volar sobre la nieve
tendremos que pacer sin descanso las hierbas de los cementerios.

Nueva York, 10 de enero de 1930

146

II. LITTLE INFINITE POEM

For Luis Cardoza y Aragón

Mistaking the way,
we come upon snow,
and coming on snow,
we nibble the graveyard grasses two thousand years.

Mistaking the way,
we come upon woman,
woman undaunted by light,
killer of gamecocks (two in a second)
the light undismayed by the cock,
the cock wanting cunning to sing in the snow.

Mistaking the heart, the snow
brings a wind from the South,
wind with no care for our weeping;
and the graveyard grasses are ours to nibble again.

Two wan, waxen wheat-staves I saw
that buried a landscape's volcanoes;
two idiot children that leaned on a murderer's eyeballs, and
      groaned.

But two is no quantity;
two is anguish, perhaps, and its shadow,
desperation's guitar for the loving,
another infinity's witness, but never its own.
Death's stronghold is two,
and the lash of a new resurrection, world without end.
Two is abhorred by the dead,
but woman is lulled by a two,
woman timid in daylight,
light flinching in cock-crow,
the cock knowing only its flight over snow,
while we nibble the graveyard grasses again, unappeased.

New York, January 10, 1930

III. SUICIDE IN ALEXANDRIA[1]

13 and 22

When the severed head was placed on the office table, it blew out the panes of the city. We must calm all these roses, the old lady said. An auto went by: Number 13. Another went by: Number 22. A shop: Number 13. A kilometer: Number 22. The situation by now was insufferable. Nothing for it, but to break off for good.

12 and 21

After the terrible rites, everyone climbed up to the topmost blade of the thistle; but the ant proved so mighty, so mighty, it had to keep to the ground with the hammer and the threaded eye of the needle.

11 and 20

Then they were off in an automobile. To make an end of it, to set an example, to make sure not a single canoe would get close to the shore.

10 and 19

They smashed the partitions and fluttered their handkerchiefs. Genevieve! Genevieve! Genevieve! Night fell; the tooth and the whip were essential.

9 and 18

So they ended it all, as they had to—or rather, we all ended it all. My love and my darling! The Eiffel Tower is superb, and so is the sombre Thames. If we go to Lord Butown's, they will serve us a lobster-head and a smoke-ring. But nobody will be going to visit the Chilenean.

8 and 17

No help for it now. Kiss me quick, but don't wrinkle my tie. Kiss me quick, kiss me quick.

17 and 16

I, a child, and you, whom the sea favors. Let me concede that the right cheek is a patternless world, and astronomy, a sliver of soap.

6 and 15

Goodbye, all! Help! Help! Darling, my darling! We both died together. For pity's sake, make an end of this poem.

5 and 14

4 and 13

When the moment arrived we saw all the lovers embracing out on the waves.

3 and 12

2 and 11

1 and 10

The wildest sea-swell of all swept over the wharves and covered the boats. Only a strangled voice could be heard, crying out from the fish.

9

8

7

6

5

4

3

2

1

0

Shall we ever forget, we summer folk there on the Alexandrian coast, the sad little love scene that brought tears to all eyes!

1928

IV. SWIMMER SUBMERGED

*Little tribute to a
society columnist.*

I was in love with two ladies who did not return my affection, but I still saw no reason for doing my favorite dog in. Doesn't it strike you, Countess, I took the noblest way out?

Now I know what it means to say farewell forever. The daily embrace reeks of mollusc.

My darling's parting embrace was so perfect that people cautiously locked up their balconies. Countess, don't make me tell all. I still have a passion for a lady who caches one half of her body in the northern snows. A lady kindly to dogs, but essentially hostile to me.

I never could kiss her as I wanted to. She turned out the lights or dissolved in a whiskey flask. And I never could fancy English gin at the time; so imagine the state of my misery, friend!

One night, the devil played hob with my shoes. It was three in the morning. I lay with a surgical knife in my throat, and she, with an out-size handkerchief. My mistake. With a horse's tail. The invisible horse by whose tail I was dragged through the streets. Countess, you do well to keep squeezing my hand.

We began to talk it all out. I laid open a gash in my forehead, and she neatly splintered the pane of her cheek. We fell into each other's arms.

You know all the rest.

A faraway orchestra struggled dramatically with flying ants.

Madame Barthou made the night irresistible with her languishing diamonds (from Cairo) and with every passing minute, the violet gown of Olga Montcha betrayed her passion for the dead Tzar.

150

Margarita Gross and Lola Cabeza de Vaca, than whom no one could be Spanisher, counted well over a thousand waves, but without much result.

On the seacoast of France, those who pilfer the fisherman's salt and murder the sailors, broke into song.

Countess: that final embrace had three tempi and was admirably managed.

Since then, I have abandoned the old literatures I had cultivated so very successfully.

One must break it all up; the dogmas must clean themselves up and the patterns take on new excitement.

Partridge-eyes for the elephant, and unicorn hooves for the partridge.

An embrace has taught me these things, and a passion has slashed my silk waistcoat.

"Do you hear that American waltz? In Vienna there is all too much almond *glacé*, too much intellectualism. The American waltz is just right: like a Naval Academy. Would you care for a turn on the dance floor?"

*

The following morning, the Countess of X was found on the beach with an absinthe fork driven into her nape. Death must have been instantaneous. On the sand, was a blood-stained piece of paper, reading: "Since you can't be a dove, you are better off dead."

The police rode up and down the dunes on their bicycles. It was ascertained that the lovely Countess of X was especially fond of swimming, and that she met her death by this means.

In any case, the name of her marvelous assailant went unknown; we will vouch for that.

1928

V. LOVERS SLAIN BY A PARTRIDGE

Homage to Guy de Maupassant

"Both of them wanted it," his mother told me.

Both of them. "That's impossible, madam," I said. "You are much too impressionable; you've too little ivy to cover your eyes. (Quiet there, Luciano, be quiet!)"

To contend with that name, one would have to prevail over bottles of anise. Do you think that a fragment of denture or a child's hand forgetfully left to the wave could comfort my wretchedness? "Both of them wanted it," his cousin assured me. "Both of them."

My favorite cricket blanked its 40 thousand eyes. 40, forty. Little girl, little girl! Little man, little man! Little ñ of my eyes. Little ñ in the distance. Can it be that this pallor of trans-ocean liners, moon-whitened, could break from the beak of the cruelest dove with an elephant's heart?

The wolves on the uplands loved it. The fault isn't mine. Nor the windflower. See—I'm in tears!

Both of them wanted it, I said. Both of them. Apples may always be lovers, but lovers are never like apples.

That's why they died. That's it, exactly. With twenty rivers and a single, dismembered winter.

It was all very easy. They loved one another despite all the museums. The right with the left hand. The left with the right hand. The right with the right foot. The left foot with a cloud. The hair of the head with the sole of the foot. The sole of the foot with the left cheek. That left cheek! Northwester of dories and quicksilver ants! Pass me the handkerchief, Genevieve; I'll have a good cry. With an *A* and an *E* and an *I* knifing into my throat. They all went to bed. Never was scene more affecting. The left thigh with the left forearm. Shut-eyed, with fingernails open. Waist with the nape of the neck and a shoreline. And four little ears with four angels in a cabin of snow. They lusted. They loved. Gravity's law notwithstanding. The difference between Stars and the spines of a rose—nothing simpler! When they discovered the facts for them-selves they went out in the open. Both were in love. Good Lord, they even made love in the presence of chemists. Shoulder to earth, earth into anise-seed. Hands with seventeen fingers or more. A rosy line ran from the heart to the tooth-line, and the little dog left alone in the RR, lost four of his paws. But they both were in love.

A man and a woman it was; or rather, a man and a hummock of earth, an elephant and a boy, an ape and a reed. There were two indeterminate men and a leg, nickel-plated. There were boatmen. Yes, the men from the Seine who smashed the world's roses to pulp.

But both were in love. And loving, as everyone knows now, is splitting the pod of the almond with all possible care and no harm to the fruit of our neighbor.

That's how it happened. So the newspapers said. We read of it, by the flare of gillettes.

On the isles of the Azores. I'm past weeping now, almost. When I sent off the wire it was late.

Late. Very late.

This, my dear Captain, is the cause of my odd melancholia.

1926-1928(?)

VI. THE DUENDE: [1] THEORY AND DIVERTISSEMENT

Composed and delivered by Lorca during his stay in Havana en route from the United States; subsequently repeated in Buenos Aires for the Sociedad Amigos del Arte (1934).

Whoever inhabits that bull's hide stretched between the Jucar, the Guadalete, the Sil, or the Pisuerga[2]—no need to mention the streams joining those lion-colored waves churned up by the Plata— has heard it said with a certain frequency: "Now that has real *duende!*" It was in this spirit that Manuel Torres, that great artist of the Andalusian people, once remarked to a singer: "You have a voice, you know all the styles, but you will never bring it off because you have no *duende.*"

In all Andalusia, from the rock of Jaen to the shell of Cádiz, people constantly speak of the *duende* and find it in everything that springs out of energetic instinct. That marvelous singer, "El Librijano," originator of the *Debla,* observed, "Whenever I am singing with *duende,* no one can come up to me"; and one day the old gypsy dancer, "La Malena," exclaimed while listening to Brailowsky play a fragment of Bach: "Olé! That has *duende!*"—and remained bored by Gluck and Brahms and Darius Milhaud. And Manuel Torres, to my mind a man of exemplary blood culture, once uttered this splendid phrase while listening to Falla himself play his "Nocturno del Generalife": "Whatever has black sounds, has *duende.*" There is no greater truth.

These "black sounds" are the mystery, the roots that probe through the mire that we all know of, and do not understand, but which furnishes us with whatever is sustaining in art. Black sounds: so said the celebrated Spaniard, thereby concurring with Goethe, who, in effect, defined the *duende* when he said, speaking of Paganini: "A mysterious power that all may feel and no philosophy can explain."

The *duende,* then, is a power and not a construct, is a struggle and not a concept. I have heard an old guitarist, a true virtuoso, remark, "The *duende* is not in the throat, the *duende* comes up from inside, up from the very soles of the feet." That is to say, it is not a question of aptitude, but of a true and viable style—of blood, in other words; of what is oldest in culture: of creation made act.

This "mysterious power that all may feel and no philosophy can explain," is, in sum, the earth-force, the same *duende* that fired the heart of Nietzsche, who sought it in its external forms on the Rialto Bridge, or in the music of Bizet, without ever finding it, or understanding that the *duende* he pursued had rebounded from the mystery-minded Greeks to the dancers of Cádiz or the gored, Dionysian cry of Silverio's *siguiriya*.[3]

So much for the *duende;* but I would not have you confuse the *duende* with the theological demon of doubt at whom Luther, on a Bacchic impulse, hurled an inkwell in Nuremberg,[4] or with the Catholic devil, destructive, but short on intelligence, who disguised himself as a bitch in order to enter the convents, or with the talking monkey that Cervantes' mountebank carried in the comedy about jealousy and the forests of Andalusia.[5]

No. The *duende* I speak of, shadowy, palpitating, is a descendant of that benignest daemon of Socrates, he of marble and salt, who scratched the master angrily the day he drank the hemlock; and of that melancholy imp of Descartes, little as an unripe almond, who, glutted with circles and lines, went out on the canals to hear the drunken sailors singing.

Any man—any artist, as Nietzsche would say—climbs the stairway in the tower of his perfection at the cost of a struggle with a *duende* —not with an angel, as some have maintained, or with his muse. This fundamental distinction must be kept in mind if the root of a work of art is to be grasped.

The Angel guides and endows, like Saint Raphael, or prohibits and avoids like Saint Michael, or foretells, like Saint Gabriel.

The Angel dazzles; but he flies over men's heads and remains in mid-air, shedding his grace; and the man, without any effort whatever, realizes his work, or his fellow-feeling, or his dance. The angel on the road to Damascus, and he who entered the crevice of the little balcony of Assisi, or that other angel who followed in the footsteps of Heinrich Suso,[6] *commanded*—and there was no resisting his radiance, for he waved wings of steel in an atmosphere of predestination.

The Muse dictates and, in certain cases, prompts. There is relatively little she can do, for she keeps aloof and is so full of lassitude (I have seen her twice) that I myself have had to put half a heart of marble in her. The Poets of the Muse hear voices and do not know where they come from; but surely they are from the Muse, who encourages and at times devours them entirely. Such, for example, was the case of Apollinaire, that great poet ravaged by the horrible Muse with whom the divinely angelic Rousseau painted him. The Muse arouses the intellect, bearing landscapes of columns and the false taste of laurel; but intellect is oftentimes the foe of poetry because it imitates too much: it elevates the poet to a throne of acute angles and makes him forget that in time the ants can devour him, too, or that a great, arsenical locust can fall on his head, against which the Muses who live inside monocles or the lukewarm lacquer roses of insignificant salons, are helpless.

Angel and Muse approach from without; the Angel sheds light and the Muse gives form (Hesiod learned of them). Gold leaf or chiton-folds: the poet finds his models in his laurel coppice. But the *Duende,* on the other hand, must come to life in the nethermost recesses of the blood.

And repel the Angel, too—kick out the Muse and conquer his awe of the fragrance of the violets that breathe from the poetry of the eighteenth century, or of the great telescope in whose lenses the Muse dozes off, sick of limits.

The true struggle is with the *Duende.*

The paths leading to God are well known, from the barbaric way of the hermit, to the subtler modes of the mystic. With a tower, then, like Saint Theresa, or with three roads, like St. John of the Cross. And even if we must cry out in Isaiah's voice: "Truly, thou art the hidden God!" at the end and at last, God sends to each seeker his first fiery thorns.

To seek out the *Duende,* however, neither map nor discipline is required. Enough to know that he kindles the blood like an irritant, that he exhausts, that he repulses, all the bland, geometrical assurances, that he smashes the styles; that he makes of a Goya, master of the grays, the silvers, the roses of the great English painters, a man painting with his knees and his fists in bituminous blacks; that he bares a Mosen Cinto Verdaguer[7] to the cold of the Pyrenees or induces a Jorge Manrique[8] to sweat out his death on the crags of Ocaña, or invests the delicate body of Rimbaud in the green domino of the saltimbanque, or fixes dead fish-eyes on the Comte de Lautréamont in the early hours of the boulevard.

The great artists of southern Spain, both gypsies and flamenco, whether singing or dancing or playing on instruments, know that no emotion is possible without the mediation of the *Duende*. They may hoodwink the people, they may give the illusion of *duende* without really having it, just as writers and painters and literary fashion-mongers without *duende* cheat you daily; but it needs only a little care and the will to resist one's own indifference, to discover the imposture and put it and its crude artifice to flight.

Once the Andalusian singer, Pastora Pavon, "The Girl with the Combs," a sombre Hispanic genius whose capacity for fantasy equals Goya's or Raphael el Gallo's, was singing in a little tavern in Cádiz. She sparred with her voice—now shadowy, now like molten tin, now covered over with moss; she tangled her voice in her long hair or drenched it in sherry or lost it in the darkest and furthermost bramble bushes. But nothing happened—useless, all of it! The hearers remained silent.

There stood Ignacio Espeleta, handsome as a Roman turtle, who was asked once why he never worked, and replied with a smile worthy of Argantonio: "How am I to work if I come from Cádiz?"

There, too, stood Héloise, the fiery aristocrat, whore of Seville, direct descendant of Soledad Vargas, who in the thirties refused to marry a Rothschild because he was not of equal blood. There were the Floridas, whom some people call butchers, but who are really millennial priests sacrificing bulls constantly to Geryon; and in a corner stood that imposing breeder of bulls, Don Pablo Murabe, with the air of a Cretan mask. Pastora Pavon finished singing in the midst of total silence. There was only a little man, one of those dancing mannikins who leap suddenly out of brandy bottles, who observed sarcastically in a very low voice: *"Viva Paris!"* As if to say: We are not interested in aptitude or techniques or virtuosity here. We are interested in something else.

Then the "Girl with the Combs" got up like a woman possessed, her face blasted like a medieval weeper, tossed off a great glass of Cazalla at a single draught, like a potion of fire, and settled down to singing—without a voice, without breath, without nuance, throat aflame—but with *duende!* She had contrived to annihilate all that was nonessential in song and make way for an angry and incandescent *Duende,* friend of the sand-laden winds, so that everyone listening tore at his clothing almost in the same rhythm with which the West Indian negroes in their rites rend away their clothes, huddled in heaps before the image of Saint Barbara.

The "Girl with the Combs" had to *mangle* her voice because she knew there were discriminating folk about who asked not for form, but for the marrow of form—pure music spare enough to keep itself in air. She had to deny her faculties and her security; that is to say, to turn out her Muse and keep vulnerable, so that her *Duende* might come and vouchsafe the hand-to-hand struggle. And then how she sang! Her voice feinted no longer; it jetted up like blood, ennobled by sorrow and sincerity, it opened up like ten fingers of a hand around the nailed feet of a Christ by Juan de Juni[9]—tempestuous!

The arrival of the *Duende* always presupposes a radical change in all the forms as they existed on the old plane. It gives a sense of refreshment unknown until then, together with that quality of the just-opening rose, of the miraculous, which comes and instils an almost religious transport.

In all Arabian music, in the dances, songs, elegies of Arabia, the coming of the *Duende* is greeted by fervent outcries of *Allah! Allah! God! God!,* so close to the *Olé! Olé!* of our bull rings that who is to say they are not actually the same; and in all the songs of southern Spain the appearance of the *Duende* is followed by heartfelt exclamations of *God alive!*—profound, human, tender, the cry of communion with God through the medium of the five senses and the grace of the *Duende* that stirs the voice and the body of the dancer—a flight from this world, both real and poetic, pure as Pedro Soto de Roja's over the seven gardens (that most curious poet of the seventeenth century), or Juan Calimacho's on the tremulous ladder of tears.

Naturally, when flight is achieved, all feel its effects: the initiate coming to see at last how style triumphs over inferior matter, and the unenlightened, through the I-don't-know-what of an authentic emotion. Some years ago, in a dancing contest at Jerez de la Frontera, an old lady of eighty, competing against beautiful women and young girls with waists supple as water, carried off the prize merely by the act of raising her arms, throwing back her head, and stamping the little platform with a blow of her feet; but in the conclave of muses and angels foregathered there—beauties of form and beauties of smile—the dying *Duende* triumphed as it had to, trailing the rusted knife blades of its wings along the ground.

All the arts are capable of *duende,* but it naturally achieves its widest play in the fields of music, dance, and the spoken poem, since these require a living presence to interpret them, because they are forms which grow and decline perpetually and raise their contours on the precise present.

Often the *Duende* of the musician passes over into the *Duende* of the interpreter, and at other times, when musician and poet are not matched, the *Duende* of the interpreter—this is interesting—creates a new marvel that retains the appearance—and the appearance only—of the originating form. Such was the case with the *duende*-ridden Duse who deliberately sought out failures in order to turn them into triumphs, thanks to her capacity for invention; or with Paganini who, as Goethe explained, could make one hear profoundest melody in out-and-out vulgarity; or with a delectable young lady from the port of Santa María whom I saw singing and dancing the horrendous Italian ditty, "O Marie!" with such rhythms, such pauses, and such conviction that she transformed an Italian gewgaw into a hard serpent of raised gold. What happened, in effect, was that each in his own way found something new, something never before encountered, which put lifeblood and art into bodies void of expression.

In every country, death comes as a finality. It comes, and the curtain comes down. But not in Spain! In Spain the curtain goes up. Many people live out their lives between walls till the day they die and are brought out into the sun. In Spain, the dead are more alive than the dead of any other country of the world: their profile wounds like the edge of a barber's razor. The quip about death and the silent contemplation of it are familiar to the Spanish. From the "Dream of the Skulls" of Quevedo,[10] to the "Putrescent Bishop" of Valdés Leal;[11] from La Marbella of the seventeenth century who, dying in childbirth on the highway, says:

> The blood of my entrails
> Covers the horse.
> And the horses' hooves
> Strike fire from the pitch.

to a recent young man from Salamanca, killed by a bull, who exclaimed:

> My friends, I am dying.
> My friends, it goes badly.
> I've three handkerchiefs inside me,
> And this I apply now makes four.

there is a balustrade of flowering nitre where hordes peer out, contemplating death, with verses from Jeremiah for the grimmer side or sweet-smelling cypress for the more lyrical—but in any case, a country where all that is most important has its final metallic valuation in death.

The knife and the cart wheel and the razor and the stinging beard-points of the shepherds, the shorn moon and the fly, the damp lockers, the ruins and the lace-covered saints, the quicklime and the cutting line of eaves and balconies: in Spain, all bear little grass-blades of death, allusions and voices perceptible to the spiritually alert, that call to our memory with the corpse-cold air of our own passing. It is no accident that all Spanish art is bound to our soil, so full of thistles and definitive stone; the lamentations of Pleberio or the dances of the master Josef Maria de Valdivielso are not isolated instances, nor is it by chance that from all the balladry of Europe the Spanish inamorata disengages herself in this fashion:

> "If you are my fine friend,
> Tell me—why won't you look at me?"
>> "The eyes with which I look at you
>> I gave up to the shadow."
> "If you are my fine friend
> Tell me—why don't you kiss me?"
>> "The lips with which I kissed you
>> I gave up to the clay."
> "If you are my fine friend
> Tell me—why won't you embrace me?"
>> **"The arms that embrace you
>> I have covered up with worms."**

Nor is it strange to find that in the dawn of our lyricism, the following note is sounded:

> Inside the garden
> I shall surely die.
> Inside the rosebush
> They will kill me.
> Mother, Mother, I went out
> Gathering roses,
> But surely death will find me
> In the garden.
> Mother, Mother, I went out
> Cutting roses,
> But surely death will find me
> In the rosebush.
> Inside the garden
> I shall surely die.
> In the rosebush
> They will kill me.

Those heads frozen by the moon that Zurbarán[12] painted, the butter-yellows and the lightning-yellows of El Greco, the narrative of Father Sigüenza, all the work of Goya, the presbytery of the Church of the Escorial, all polychrome sculpture, the crypt of the ducal house of Osuna, the death with the guitar in the chapel of the Benavente in Medina de Río Seco—all equal, on the plane of cultivated art, the pilgrimages of San Andrés de Teixido where the dead have their place in the procession; they are one with the songs for the dead that the women of Asturias intone with flame-filled lamps in the November night, one with the song and dance of the Sibyl in the cathedrals of Mallorca and Toledo, with the obscure "In Recort" of Tortosa, and the innumerable rites of Good Friday that, with the arcane Fiesta of the Bulls, epitomize the popular triumph of Spanish death. In all the world, Mexico alone can go hand-in-hand with my country.

When the Muse sees death on the way, she closes the door, or raises a plinth, or promenades an urn and inscribes an epitaph with a waxen hand, but in time she tears down her laurels again in a silence that wavers between two breezes. Under the truncated arch of the Ode, she joins with funereal meaning the exact flowers that the Italians of the fifteenth century depicted, with the identical cock of Lucretius, to frighten off an unforeseen darkness.

When the Angel sees death on the way, he flies in slow circles and weaves with tears of narcissus and ice the elegy we see trembling in the hands of Keats and Villasandino[13] and Herrera[14] and Becquer[15] and Juan Ramón Jiménez.[16] But imagine the terror of the Angel, should it feel a spider—even the very tiniest—on its tender and roseate flesh!

The *Duende,* on the other hand, will not approach at all if he does not see the possibility of death, if he is not convinced he will circle death's house, if there is not every assurance he can rustle the branches borne aloft by us all, that neither have, nor may ever have, the power to console.

With idea, with sound, or with gesture, the *Duende* chooses the brim of the well for his open struggle with the creator. Angel and Muse escape in the violin or in musical measure, but the *Duende* draws blood, and in the healing of the wound that never quite closes, all that is unprecedented and invented in a man's work has its origin.

The magical virtue of poetry lies in the fact that it is always empowered with *duende* to baptize in dark water all those who behold it, because with *duende,* loving and understanding are simpler, there is always the *certainty* of being loved and being understood; and this struggle for expression and for the communication of expression acquires at times, in poetry, finite characters.

Recall the case of that paragon of the flamenco and daemonic way, Saint Theresa—flamenca not for her prowess in stopping an angry bull with three magnificent passes—though she did so—nor for her presumption in esteeming herself beautiful in the presence of Fray Juan de la Miseria, nor for slapping the face of a papal nuncio; but rather for the simple circumstance that she was one of the rare ones whose *Duende* (not her Angel—the angels never attack) pierced her with an arrow, hoping thereby to destroy her for having deprived him of his ultimate secret: the subtle bridge that links the five senses with the very center, the living flesh, living cloud, living sea, of Love emancipated from Time.

Most redoubtable conqueress of the *Duende*—and how utterly unlike the case of Philip of Austria who, longing to discover the Muse and the Angel in theology, found himself imprisoned by the *Duende* of cold ardors in that masterwork of the Escorial, where geometry abuts with a dream and the *Duende* wears the mask of the Muse for the eternal chastisement of the great king.

We have said that the *Duende* loves ledges and wounds, that he enters only those areas where form dissolves in a passion transcending any of its visible expressions.

In Spain (as in all Oriental countries where dance is a form of religious expression) the *Duende* has unlimited play in the bodies of the dancers of Cádiz, eulogized by Martial, in the breasts of the singers, eulogized by Juvenal, and in all the liturgy of the bulls—that authentic religious drama where, in the manner of the Mass, adoration and sacrifice are rendered a God.

It would seem that all the *duende* of the classical world is crowded into this matchless festival, epitomizing the culture and the noble sensibility of a people who discover in man his greatest rages, his greatest melancholies, his greatest lamentations. No one, I think, is amused by the dances or the bulls of Spain; the *Duende* has taken it on himself to make them suffer through the medium of the drama, in living forms, and prepares the ladders for a flight from encompassing reality.

The *Duende* works on the body of the dancer like wind works on sand. With magical force, it converts a young girl into a lunar paralytic; or fills with adolescent blushes a ragged old man begging handouts in the wineshops; or suddenly discovers the smell of nocturnal ports in a head of hair, and moment for moment, works on the arms with an expressiveness which is the mother of the dance of all ages.

But it is impossible for him ever to repeat himself—this is interesting and must be underscored. The *Duende* never repeats himself, any more than the forms of the sea repeat themselves in a storm.

In the bullfight, the *Duende* achieves his most impressive advantage, for he must fight then with death who can destroy him, on one hand, and with geometry, with measure, the fundamental basis of the bullfight, on the other.

The bull has his orbit, and the bullfighter has his, and between orbit and orbit is the point of risk where falls the vertex of the terrible byplay.

It is possible to hold a Muse with a *muleta*[17] and an Angel with *banderillas*,[18] and pass for a good bullfighter; but for the *faena de capa*,[19] with the bull still unscarred by a wound, the help of the *Duende* is necessary at the moment of the kill, to drive home the blow of artistic truth.

The bullfighter who moves the public to terror in the plaza by his audacity does not *fight* the bull—that would be ludicrous in such a case—but, within the reach of each man, puts his life at stake; on the contrary, the fighter bitten by the *Duende* gives a lesson in Pythagorean music and induces all to forget how he constantly hurls his heart against the horns.

Lagartijo with his Roman *duende,* Joselito with his Jewish *duende,* Belmonte with his baroque *duende,* and Cagancho with his gypsy *duende,* from the twilight of the ring, teach poets, painters, and musicians four great ways of the Spanish tradition.

Spain is the only country where death is the national spectacle, where death blows long fanfares at the coming of each Spring, and its art is always governed by a shrewd *duende* that has given it its distinctive character and its quality of invention.

The *Duende* that, for the first time in sculpture, fills the cheeks of the saints of the master Mateo de Compostela with blood, is the same spirit that evokes the lamentations of St. John of the Cross or burns naked nymphs on the religious sonnets of Lope.

The *Duende* who raises the tower of Sahagun or tesselates hot brick in Calatayud or Teruel, is the same spirit that breaks open the clouds of El Greco and sends the constables of Quevedo and the chimaeras of Goya sprawling with a kick.

When it rains, he secretly brings out a *duende*-minded Velasquez, behind his monarchical grays; when it snows, he sends Herrera out naked to prove that cold need not kill; when it burns, he casts Berruguete [20] into the flames and lets him invent a new space for sculpture.

The Muse of Góngora and the Angel of Garcilaso [21] must yield up the laurel wreath when the *Duende* of St. John of the Cross passes by, when

> The wounded stag
> peers over the hill.

The Muse of Gonzalo de Berceo [22] and the Angel of the Archpriest of Hita [23] must give way to the approaching Jorge Manrique when he comes, wounded to death, to the gates of the Castle of Belmonte. The Muse of Gregorio Hernandez [24] and the Angel of José de Mora [25] must retire, so that the *Duende* weeping blood-tears of Mena, [26] and the *Duende* of Martínez Montañes [27] with a head like an Assyrian bull's, may pass over, just as the melancholy Muse of Cataluña and the humid Angel of Galicia must watch, with loving terror, the *Duende* of Castile, far from the hot bread and the cow grazing mildly among forms of swept sky and parched earth.

The *Duende* of Quevedo and the *Duende* of Cervantes, one bearing phosphorescent green anemones and the other the plaster flowers of Ruidera, crown the altar-piece of the *Duende* of Spain.

Each art has, by nature, its distinctive *Duende* of style and form, but all roots join at the point where the black sounds of Manuel Torres issue forth—the ultimate stuff and the common basis, uncontrollable and tremulous, of wood and sound and canvas and word.

Black sounds: behind which there abide, in tenderest intimacy, the volcanoes, the ants, the zephyrs, and the enormous night straining its waist against the Milky Way.

165

Ladies and gentlemen: I have raised three arches, and wit[ ]
clumsy hand I have placed in them the Muse, the Angel, and th[ ]
Duende.

The Muse keeps silent; she may wear the tunic of little fold[ ]
or great cow-eyes gazing toward Pompeii, or the monstrous, four[ ]
featured nose with which her great painter, Picasso, has painted he[ ]
The Angel may be stirring the hair of Antonello da Messina,[28] th[ ]
tunic of Lippi,[29] and the violin of Masolino[30] or Rousseau.[31]

But the Duende—where is the Duende? Through the empty arc[ ]
enters a mental air blowing insistently over the heads of the dea[ ]
seeking new landscapes and unfamiliar accents; an air bearing th[ ]
odor of child's spittle, crushed grass, and the veil of a Medusa ar[ ]
nouncing the unending baptism of all newly-created things.

193[ ]

VII. THE POETIC IMAGE IN DON LUIS DE GÓNGORA

Composed and delivered in Granada, on the occasion of the tercentenary of Góngora; repeated at the Residencia de Estudiantes in Madrid; published by the Residencia in 1932 and in "Cursos y Conferencias," Buenos Aires, November, 1936.

At the outset, I assume that you are aware who Don Luis de Góngora was, and what is meant by a poetic image. You have all studied Rhetoric and the History of Literature, and your teachers, with rare and recent exceptions, have told you that though Góngora was a very fine poet, he quite suddenly, for a number of reasons, transformed himself into a very eccentric one (from an "angel of light" to an "angel of darkness," is the accepted formula); and that he carried language and rhythm to extremes of distortion inconceivable to well-balanced minds. These notions have been aired in the high schools, while there has been praise for the insipidities of Núñez de Arce,[1] for the journalistic esthetic—the weddings, baptisms, burials, and railway journeys—of Campoamor,[2] or for the mediocre Zorilla[3] (not the magnificent Zorilla of the plays and legends). My own teacher is a case in point: he declaimed him while pacing up and down before the class, and ended with his tongue hanging out, amidst the hilarity of the small fry.

Góngora has been abused in pique and defended with ardor. Yet today his work vibrates as though still fresh from the creative act; and though a murmur of contention still surrounds his true glory, it is now a little crestfallen.

A poetic image is always a transference of meaning.

At the basis of all language is the image, and our people have been especially prodigal in these. To call the projecting element of a roof an *alero*[4] is a magnificent image; to call a confection *bacon of heaven* and another *nun's sigh,* is a shrewd and engaging conceit; to call a cupola a *half-orange,* is another; and so on. In Andalusia, folk imagery reaches an epitome of refinement and sensibility; and these transmutations are wholly Gongoristic.

To a deep waterway that flows slowly through a field, the name of *water-ox*[5] is given to suggest its volume, its pressure, and its power; and I have heard a farmer from Granada say: "Rushes always love to grow in the *tongue* of the river." *Water-ox* and *tongue of the river* are two instances of folk imagery very closely allied to Góngora's characteristic manner.

To place Góngora in his world, we must first take note of two schools of poetry struggling for mastery in the history of Spanish lyricism: the so-called "popular"—or the more improperly called "national" poets—and the poets rightly known as cultivated or courtly: those who make their poems on the road, and those who write them seated at a table, watching the roadside through the leaded glass of the window. While the indigenous—and anonymous— poets of the thirteenth century stammered songs medieval in feeling, in the Galician and Castilian modes, songs unfortunately now lost, the school that we are going to call the "opposite" school, to distinguish it from the others, turned its attention to the French and Provençal. Under that humid and golden sky, there came to light the *cancioneros* of Ajuda and the Vatican,[6] where, over the Provençal lyrics of King Dinis and the cultivated *canciones de amigo* or *cantigas de amor,* we can hear the delicate voices of anonymous poets singing a pure song unfettered by grammar and unawed by the forms so highly esteemed in the Middle Ages. . . .

The eminent Menéndez Pidal[7] has said that humanism "opened" the eyes of the scholar to a more considered understanding of the human spirit in all its aspects, and that the popular tradition deserves honorable and intelligent scrutiny—which, up to now, it has not received. Proof of this can be seen in the cultivation of the guitar and the folk song by great musicians like Valencia's Luis Milán, that gifted emulator of Castiglione's *Courtier,* and Francisco Salinas, the Friend of Fray Luis de León.

Open war was declared between the two schools. Cristóbal de Castillejo[8] and Gregorio Silvestre,[9] with their love of the popular tradition, carried the Castilian standard. Garcilaso, followed by a more numerous band, declared for the so-called Italianate taste. And when, in the last months of 1609, Góngora wrote his *Panegírico al Duque de Lerma,* the battle between the partizans of the refined style and the friends of the indefatigable Lope de Vega[10] reached a point of temerity and hysteria unparalleled in literary history. The partizans of the "dark" Góngora and of the "light" Góngora waged a lively and diverting war of sonnets, at times dramatic, but almost always ribald.

But I should like to make clear that I do not believe this struggle produced any noteworthy result; I hold no brief for either the Italianate or the Castilian school. As I see it, both schools are capable of a profound national feeling. The foreign influence is unquestionable, of course, but it did not weigh down their spirits. All such classifications are a matter of historical perspective. Garcilaso is as national a poet as Castillejo. Castillejo is imbued with the spirit of the Middle Ages; but he is an "archaist" only by reason of his fondness for a recently terminated mode. Garcilaso, a Renaissance mind, unearths on the beaches of the Tajo old mythologies beclouded by time, but he brings to them a genuinely national elegance that is part of his time, and a mode of expression indestructibly Spanish.

In culling the archaic lyrics of the waning Middle Ages and creating a profoundly romantic theater, Lope was similarly a child of his age. He received the full brunt of the great maritime discoveries, in all their relative recency—pure romanticism! His theater of love, of adventure and the duel, proves him a man in the national tradition. But Góngora was no less national than Lope. Góngora shunned, in his characteristic and definitive work, the chivalric tradition, as well as the medieval, seeking—not superficially, like Garcilaso, but profoundly—the glories of the old Latin tradition. In the lonely air of Córdova, he seeks the voices of Seneca and Lucan. And molding Castilian verse by the cold light of the Roman lamp, he raises to its highest power a genre of art uniquely Spanish in character: the baroque. There was heated dissension between medievalists and Latinists—the poets with a preference for the picturesque and the local, and the poets of the court. The poets that go muffled, and the poets who prefer nakedness. But the ordered and sensuous atmosphere demanded by the Italian Renaissance never found its way to their hearts. They were either romantics, like Lope and Herrera, or distinctly Catholic and baroque in sentiment, like Góngora and Calderón. Geography and Heaven triumphed over the Library.

2.

I should like to leave this brief resumé at this point. I have been concerned only to trace out the line of Góngora and set the master in his aristocratic solitude.

"Much has been written about Góngora, but still the genesis of his poetic reforms remains dark." So the wariest and the most venturesome grammarians begin, when speaking of the father of modern lyricism. I will not mention by name Menéndez y Pelayo,[11] who never understood Góngora at all—because, on the contrary, he understood everybody else so well. There are those who refer what they call the abrupt change of Don Luis de Góngora, with certain historical justification, to the theories of Ambrosio de Morales, to the suggestions of his teacher, Herrera, or his reading of Luis Carillo (his defense of obscurity in style), and other plausible causes. Then there is a Frenchman, M. Lucien Paul Thomas, who attributes it to a brain disorder, while Mr. Fitzmaurice Kelly, demonstrating the critical ineptitude that marks him whenever he is coping with an unclassifiable author, is inclined to believe that the aim of the author of *Soledades* was merely to draw attention to his literary personality. Is there anything more picturesque than these *solemn* animadversions—or more profane?

In Spain, the Góngora *culterano* was considered—and still is, to a large nucleus of opinion—a monster of grammatical vices whose poetry lacks every element requisite to beauty. The *Soledades* have been regarded by the most celebrated grammarians and rhetoricians as a blemish to be covered up, and there is a hue and cry of muddled and indolent voices, voices without energy or insight, that anathematize all that they call empty and obscure. They have succeeded not only in ostracizing Góngora, but in throwing dust in the eyes of later readers who have come to understand him throughout the two long centuries in which we have been warned repeatedly: "Do not come closer: the man is unintelligible." And Góngora has stood alone like a leper, covered with sores, in a cold, silver light, with the greenest of boughs in his hands, awaiting the new generations who will revive his full legacy and his feeling for metaphor.

It is a question of understanding. One must study Góngora, as well as read him. Góngora does not come soliciting us, like the other poets who prey upon our melancholy; on the contrary, we must pursue him through the exercise of reason. It is quite impossible to understand him at first reading. A work of philosophy may be understood by the few alone without exposing the author to charges of obscurity. But the poetical brotherhood? By no means! this violates all precedent, or would seem to!

What reasons could Góngora have had for launching his lyrical revolution? Reasons? An innate craving for a new order of beauty led him to fashion a new language. He was from Córdova, and knew Latin as few have known it since. There is no need to probe into history, but into his soul. For the first time he invented a new way of seizing and shaping the metaphor in the Castilian tongue; he believed implicitly that the permanence of a poem depends on the quality and coalescence of its images.

Later, it was Marcel Proust who noted: "Metaphor alone gives a semblance of eternity to style."

It was a need for new beauty, a boredom with the poetical effusions of his time, that developed in Góngora a well-nigh intolerable state of critical exacerbation. In time, he came to regard poetry almost with hatred.

He could neither create poems in the old Castilian taste, nor find satisfaction in the heroic simplicity of the ballads. Viewing the spectacle of contemporary lyricism, he found it riddled with flaws, imperfections, and vulgar sentiment. All the dust of Castile filled his soul and weighed on the cassock of the prebendary.[12] He felt that the poems of his contemporaries were faulty, slovenly, and affected.

Weary of Castilian and "local color," he read his Virgil with the gratification of a man avid for refinement. His sensitivity made a microscope of his eyes. He saw his native Castilian as a language both hobbled and sparse, and with his singular esthetic instinct, began to erect a new tower out of gems and cut stones to provoke the disdain of the Castilians in their palaces of brick. He took into account the transience of human feeling and the frailty of spontaneous expression that excites only for a moment, and he rooted his beauty in metaphor purged of ephemeral realities, metaphor built in the sculpturesque mode and removed to stratospheric altitudes.

What he loved was objective beauty, beauty useless and pure, free of panic anxiety.

While others asked for bread, he demanded a daily jewel of great price. Without sensing the reality of the real, he was absolute master of poetic reality. And how did he manage to give unity and just proportion to his esthetic beliefs? He limited himself. He examined his conscience and, with his native critical genius, studied his own creative processes.

For the poet makes himself mentor of his five bodily senses—the bodily senses in the following order: sight, touch, hearing, smell, and taste. To command ideal images, he must open the doors of communication between the senses; and frequently he must superimpose his sensations at the expense of disguising his very nature. . . .

Two conditions are necessary to give life to an image: form and a range of deployment: a central nucleus and the sweeping perspective around it. The nucleus unfolds like a flower and surprises us by its strangeness, but in the radius of brightness that encircles it, we speak the flower's name and identify its perfume. Metaphor is always ordered by vision—the faculty of sight (sometimes by sublimated vision). It is vision that delimits it and renders it actual. Even the most elusive of English poets—like Keats—felt the need of limiting and delineating their metaphors and tropes; indeed, it is only his admirable plasticity that saves Keats from the perilous world of poetic hallucination. He was led to exclaim, in the end: "Only the Poem can record the dream." Sight will not suffer what is obscure to distort the image's contour, once it has taken form.

The congenitally blind cannot be plastic poets of the objective image because they have no knowledge of Nature's proportions. The blind are happiest in the realm of the mystical, where light can be infinite, a landscape without real objects, open to the great cross-winds of wisdom.

But images unfold in the visual field.

From the sense of touch, we learn the quality of their lyric materiality; their quality—almost their picture itself. The images which the other senses compose are subordinate to the first two.

The image, then, involves a change in the garment—the functions and purposes—of objects and ideas in Nature. They have their planes and their orbits. Metaphor links two antagonistic worlds by an equestrian leap of imagination. The cinematic Jean Epstein remarks that metaphor is "that theorem in which we leap without mediation from hypothesis to conclusion." Precisely.

The originality of Don Luis de Góngora, apart from his purely grammatical inventiveness, lies in his method of *stalking the image,* perfected through studious and dramatic self-criticism. Endowed by nature with an extraordinary feeling for myth, he studied the lovely archetypes of classical cultures; and shunning the luminous vision on the heights, seated himself by the shore of the sea, where the wind

> on the blue beds of aquamarine, parted
> curtains of turquoise.

Here he reined and curbed his imagination, withdrawing like a sculptor before beginning his poem. It was his great need to command and encompass the poem that brought him, unconsciously, to a penchant for islands; for he thought, with good reason, that man could order and master the orb of earth's contour, visible and distinct in its limits of water, beyond all other land. His imaginative strategy is thus perfect; and there are times when each image is an achieved myth.

He gave harmony and plasticity to the most contradictory worlds —at times almost by violence. In his hands there is neither disorder nor dissymmetry. Like trinkets, he holds the seas, the kingdoms of earth, and the hurricane. He fuses details of the infinitesimally small with astronomic intuitions and a feeling for volume and matter unheard of in poetry until he invented them. . . . In eight lines (of *Soledades*) there is more nuance than in fifty octets of Tasso's *Jerusalem Delivered.* And this is because every detail is pondered and felt like the jewel in the goldsmith's hand. . . . Because he holds imagination in check, he can arrest it at will; he is neither wrenched by the dark forces of nature and the law of inertia, nor beguiled by the fleeting illusions in which unwary poets have perished like moths in the lamp. . . .

Of special interest is his treatment of diminutive objects and forms; for he invests both great and small with identical love and poetic sublimity. For Góngora, an apple is no less intense than the sea, a bee no less astonishing than a forest. He takes his stand before created Nature with penetrating gaze and admires an identical beauty which equates all forms. He enters what may well be called the universe of each thing and matches his sensibility with the sensations which surround it. For this reason, the apple and the sea evoke the same response; for he knows that the world of the apple is as infinite as the world of the sea. The span of the apple, from the time of its flowering till it falls from the tree to the grass in a burnish, is as great and mysterious as the measured rhythms of the tides. The poet must know this. The grandeur of verse is not determined by the magnitude of the theme or its bulk or its sentiments. Epic poems can be written about the struggle of the leucocyte in the confining network of veins, and it is possible to convey an enduring sense of the infinite in the form and fragrance of a rose.

Góngora treats all materials in the same scale; he analyses objects and fruits in the same cyclopean measure which he applies to continents and seas—and more. The smaller the thing, the more fervent his pleasure. . . .

It remained for the nineteenth century to produce the great poet and hallucinated master, Stéphane Mallarmé, who paraded his incomparable and abstract lyricism through the streets of Rome, and opened an airy and violent way to the new poetic schools. Till then, Góngora lacked for his greatest disciple—who, as it turned out, had never even read him. For they share the same love of swans, mirrors, hard high lights, feminine coiffure, the same fixed *frisson* of the baroque—with a difference, however. For Góngora not only achieves greater strength, and is marked by a verbal richness unknown to Mallarmé, but he shows an exalted sense of the beautiful that the nice humors of the moderns and the lethal point of their irony constantly suppress.

Needless to say, Góngora does not pattern his images on Nature itself; instead, he carries the object, the action, or the thing, into the darkroom of his brain, from which it issues transformed, to descend, with a leap, upon that other world with which it is merged. For this reason his poetry, by virtue of its obliquity, cannot be read in the presence of the objects to which it refers. The poplars, the roses, the shepherdesses, and the seas of his spiritual Córdova are created anew. He will call the sea a "crude emerald, ever undulant, set into marble," or a poplar a "green lyre." Nothing could be more ill-advised than to read his madrigal to a rose with an actual rose in one's hand. Either the rose or the madrigal should be more than enough.

Góngora, then, has his world apart, like all great poets: his world of the essential qualities and the characteristic differences of things.

The poet who embarks on the creation of the poem (as I know by experience), begins with the aimless sensation of a hunter about to embark on a night hunt through the remotest of forests. Unaccountable dread stirs in his heart. To reassure himself—and it is well that he do so—he drinks a glass of clear water and inscribes senseless black flourishes with his penpoint. I say black because—I say this in strictest confidence—I never use colored inks.[13] Then the poet is off on the chase. Delicate breezes chill the lenses of his eyes. The moon, curved like a horn of soft metal, calls in the silence of the topmost branches. White stags appear in the clearing between the tree trunks. Absolute night withdraws in a curtain of whispers. Water flickers in the reeds, quiet and deep. . . . It is time to depart. It is the moment of risk for the poet. He must take out his map of the terrain into which he will move and remain calm in the presence of the thousand splendors and the thousand hideous masks of the splendid that pass before his eyes. He must stop up his ears like Ulysses before the sirens and discharge all his arrows at living metaphors, avoiding all that is florid and false in their wake. The moment is hazardous if the poet at this point surrenders; should he do so, the poem would never emerge. The poet must press on to the hunt single-minded and serene; in virtual camouflage. He must stand firm in the presence of illusions and keep wary lookout for the quivering flesh of reality that accords with the shadowy map of the poem that he carries. At times, he will cry out loudly in the poem's solitude, to rout the evil spirits—facile ones who would betray us to popular adulation without order or beauty or esthetic understanding. No one was better equipped than Góngora for this interior journey. In his mind's landscape no image dismayed him, whatever the excess of brilliance or color. He stalks what none has ever seen, because none has grasped its relations—the white and truant image that animated his moments of trustful composition. His fancy drew on his five bodily senses. Unlike the run of mortals, his five senses gave blind obedience, without thought of deceit, like five guileless slaves. He intuited clearly that the Nature which issues from the hands of the Maker is not the nature that lives on in the poem, and he ordered his landscape by analysing its components. Almost it might be said that he subjects Nature and all its gradations to the discipline of musical measure. . . .

It was Paul Valéry, the great French poet, who held that the state of inspiration is not the most advantageous one for the writing of poetry. As I believe in heaven-sent inspiration, I believe that Valéry is on the right track. The inspired state is a state of self-withdrawal, and not a creative dynamism. Conceptual vision must be calmed before it can be clarified. I cannot believe that any great artist works in a fever. Even mystics return to their tasks when the ineffable dove of the Holy Ghost departs from their cells and is lost in the clouds. One returns from the inspired state as one returns from a foreign country. The poem is the legend of the journey. Inspiration furnishes the image, but not the investiture. To clothe it, it is necessary to weigh the quality and sonority of each word, coolly, and without dangerous afflatus. In Góngora, however, it is more a question of which to admire most—the poetic materials or his inspired and inimitable form. With him, the *letter* gives life to the spirit, instead of killing it. Though devoid of spontaneity, he remains youthful and fresh; though he is never simple, he is luminously intelligible. And when, as happens rarely, the result is an excess of hyperbole, it is turned with a grace so intrinsically Andalusian that we smile and admire it the more, because all his hyperbole is the extravagant compliment of a lovelorn Córdovan.

And now: as to this "obscurity" of Góngora—what does it come to? I believe there is too much illumination. Only the initiates in Poetry may approach him—those with a sensibility cultivated by reading and experience. The trespasser will never delight in his world, just as he cannot delight in a painting until he sees what is set forth by the painter; or a musical composition. Góngora is not a poet to be read, but to be loved. . . . It is we ourselves who are in darkness, who lack the wit to penetrate his intelligence. The mystery is not from without—on the contrary, we flaunt it on our hearts. Let us not speak of *obscure things,* but of *obscure people.* Góngora never wished to be murky, but elegant, various, and clear. The half-light and the misshapen metaphor were never to his taste; rather, it was his way to clarify things by encompassing them fully. He ended by giving his poems the greatness of still lives.

1927

NOTES

III. SUICIDE IN ALEXANDRIA and SWIMMER SUBMERGED

1. *Letter from Lorca to Sebastián Gasch*: "They belong to my *spiritualized* new manner, emotion disembodied and pure, disengaged from all logical control —but (mark you!) with a tremendous poetical logic. It is not surrealism— not at all—but rather the strictest self-awareness that illumines them. They are the first I've done. Naturally, they are in prose, because verse is a texture (*una ligadura*) they are not at home in. Nonetheless, you will find in them my true heart's tenderness."
The poems were published in *L'Amic de les Arts* (Sitges) September 13, 1928, with original line drawings by Lörca, nine months before his arrival in New York.

VI. THE DUENDE: THEORY AND DIVERTISSEMENT

1. The *"duende"*: Arturo Barea explains (*Lorca: The Poet and His People*): "Characteristically, Lorca took his Spanish term for daemonic inspiration from the Andalusian idiom. While to the rest of Spain the *duende* is nothing but a hobgoblin, to Andalusia it is an obscure power which can speak through every form of human art, including the art of personality."

2. *Jucar*: river of east central Spain; *Guadalete*: river in southern Spain; *Sil*: river of northwestern Spain; *Pisuerga*: river of northern Spain. *Plata*: river of South America, used by Lorca in the present context to suggest the whole of the Hispanic world outside the borders of his native Spain.

3. *Silverio's siguiriya*: Silverio Franconetti, an Italian "cantaor" who came to Seville and cultivated the "deep song" (*cante jondo*) of the Andalusian gypsy. According to Lorca, the *siguiriya* is a development of the *cante jondo* which combines elements of the primitive musical systems of India, with the indigenous folk tradition of Andalusia. The *flamenco* style, which derives from the *cante jondo*, does not take form until the eighteenth century.

4. *Nuremberg*: Lorca is apparently in error here; it was at the electoral Castle of Wartburg in Eisenach that the celebrated encounter occurred.

5. Here again Lorca is either in error, or indulging a playful hoax of his own.

6. *Heinrich Suso*: (1300-1366) German mystic and theologian.

7. *Mosen Cinto Verdaguer*: Jacinto Verdaguer (1845-1902), Catalan poet, author of *La Atlantida*.

8. *Jorge Manrique*: (1440-1479) Spanish poet and soldier, best known for the elegiac *Coplas* on his father's death.

9. *Juan de Juni*: (1507-1577) Spanish painter, pupil of Berruguete.

10. *Francisco Gomez de Quevedo y Villegas*: (1580-1654) Poet and satirist born in Madrid.

11. *Juan de Valdés Leal*: (1630-1691) Córdovan painter.
12. *Francisco de Zurbarán*: (1598-1669) Painter born in Estremadura.
13. *Alfonso Álvarez de Villasandino*: (1350?-1424?) Writer of lyric and satirical verse, born in the province of Burgos.
14. *Fernando de Herrera*: (1534-1597) Leader of the Andalusian school and innovator in the line of Góngora.
15. *Gustavo Adolfo Becquer*: (1836-1870) Romantic lyric poet born in Madrid, best known for his *Rimas*.
16. *Juan Ramón Jiménez*: (1881-19—) Contemporary lyric poet born at Moguer.
17. *Muleta*: Cloth of scarlet serge or flannel, folded and doubled over tapered wooden stick, used by matadors for defense, the positional manipulation of the bull, "passes" to demonstrate the dexterity and daring of the fighter, and as an aid in the final kill.
18. *Banderilla*: A small dart with a bannerol for baiting bulls, thrust in a series of three pairs into the withers of the bull in the second phase of the bullfight.
19. *Faena de capa*: "cape-task"; the sum of work done by matador in third phase of the fight.
20. *Alonso Berruguete*: (1490?-1581?) Baroque sculptor and architect, pupil of Michelangelo.
21. *Garcilaso de la Vega*: (1501?-1536?) Poet, statesman, and soldier, author of eclogues, elegies, and sonnets in the Italianate style.
22. *Gonzalo de Berceo*: (c. 1180-c. 1246) Early Spanish poet and Benedictine priest.
23. *Archpriest of Hita* (Juan Ruiz}: (died before 1351) Poet and priest, author of the *Libro de buen amor*.
24. *Gregorio Hernandez*: (1576-1636) Spanish sculptor born in Galicia.
25. *José de Mora*: (1638-1725) Sculptor born in Granada.
26. *Pedro de Mena*: (d. 1693) Sculptor born in Granada.
27. *Juan Martínez Montañes*: (1580-1649) Sculptor born in Granada.
28. *Antonello da Messina*: (1430-1479) Italian painter born at Messina.
29. *Fra Filippo Lippi*: (1406-1469) Italian painter and Carmelite friar born in Florence.
30. *Masolino da Panicole*: (1383-1447) Italian painter born near Florence.
31. *Henri Rousseau*: (1844-1910) The French primitive painter, whose portrait of the poet Apollinaire (*La Muse Inspirant Le Poète*) is referred to earlier in the essay.

VII. THE POETIC IMAGE IN DON LUIS DE GÓNGORA

1. *Gaspar Núñez de Arce*: (1832?-1903) Statesman and lyric poet born in Valladolid.
2. *Ramón de Campoamor*: (1817-1901) Born in Navia (Asturias), best known for his aphoristic and lapidary *Humoradas* and a Byronic poem in three cantos, *El tren expreso* (*The Express Train*).
3. *José Zorilla y Moral*: (1817-1893) Spanish romanticist, born in Valladolid, author of *Don Juan Tenorio* and legendary tales in verse; called the "last of the troubadours."

APPENDICES

4. *Alero*: Literally, *eave,* or *gable end.* The pun, and the image to which it gives rise, are untranslatable, and probably derive from *ala,* or *wing.*

5. *Water-ox*: a literal rendering of *buey de agua.* The image was a favorite one with Lorca, and its punning variation *(oso de agua* or *water-bear)* may be seen in "Christmas On the Hudson" (1. 20), where doubtless the double connotation of a jet of water and a polar (?) bear is intended.

6. *Cancioneros*: The *Cancionero de Ajuda* and the *Cancionero del Vaticano,* miscellanies of Galician and Portuguese lyric verse combining the courtly mode of King Dinis (1325) with an emergent popular tradition.

7. *Ramón Menéndez Pidal*: (1869-19—) Distinguished Hispanic scholar and student of medieval balladic literature.

8. *Cristóbal de Castillejo*: (1490-1550) Poet and Carthusian monk, author of lively love songs and anti-Italianate satires.

9. *Gregorio Silvestre Rodríguez de Mesa*: (1520-1569) Born in Lisbon, musician and convert to the Italianate lyric mode.

10. *Lope Felix de Vega Carpio*: (1562-1635) Indefatigable poet and dramatist born in Madrid, author of more than 400 extant plays and 21 volumes of non-dramatic works, and a militant adversary of Góngora.

11. *Menéndez y Pelayo*: (1856-1912) Born at Santander, professor at the University of Madrid and encyclopaedic critic and historian of Hispanic letters and civilization.

12. Góngora took orders and served variously as prebendary of the Cathedral at Córdova, priest, and chaplain to the King.

13. A playful allusion to the green inks of Pedro Salinas and the red inks of Gomez de la Serna?

POET IN NEW YORK:
A CRITICAL CHRONOLOGY

1929:
Summer

Federico García Lorca arrives in New York City, matriculates at Columbia University, and is assigned to a room in John Jay Hall.

1929:
August

By August of the same year, the *Poet in New York,* between visits to Newburg, New York and Eden Mills, Vermont, is well under way. A letter of this month from Eden Mills, confides to Ángel del Río:

> The landscape is prodigious, but infinitely sad. A good experience for me. I'll explain later . . . It never stops raining. A very likable family, full of quiet charm, but the woods and the lake have plunged me in a state of poetic desperation very hard to put up with. I write all day and by night I feel drained . . . Here comes the night. They've lighted the oil lamps and my whole childhood comes back to me, clothed in a glory of poppies and wheat. Found a distaff covered with spiders in the ferns; there's not the sound of a frog from the lake. My poor heart feels the need of a brandy . . . [I'm] hounded even to Eden Mills by the liquor of romanticism . . . It's a refuge to me, but I'm drowning in mist and tranquility—they are burning me up in my memories.

Though minor revisions continue to occupy the poet for some years to come (see variants brought together in the Appendix to the Mexican edition published by Editorial Séneca: Ediciones Arbol), the text is substantially completed by the Spring of 1930.

1930:
Spring

Lorca, in response to an invitation from the Institución Hispano-Cubana de Cultura, leaves New York for a program of lectures in Havana, where he composes the concluding "*Son* of the Negroes in Cuba."

181

1930:   *"Son* of the Negroes in Cuba," from Sect. X of *Poet in New York,* published in *Musicalia* (Havana).

1930:
Summer   Lorca leaves Cuba for Spain. To his friend, Gil Benumeya, he reports:

> I have in preparation the manuscript of four books: drama [the unfinished surrealist pieces, *Asi que pasen cinco años* and *El público?*]; verse; and a volume of New York impressions that might be called *The City*—at once a personal interpretation and a depersonalized abstraction bearing no relation in time or place to that metropolitan cosmos. A passional symbol. Of suffering. But on the other hand, without histrionics! It marks a point of contact between my own poetical world and the poetical world of New York. There between both worlds, the sad folk of Africa move in a limbo, adrift in their American setting. The Jews. And the Syrians. And the negroes. Above all, the negroes! For the spiritual axis of America has been shaped by their sadness. The negro, living close to pure human nature, and the other forces of Nature. The negro spilling music out of his pockets. Apart from the art of the negro, the United States has nothing to show but machines and automatons.

1931:   "Cow," from Sect. V, "Ruin" and "Death," from Sect VI, and "New York: Office and Denunciation," from Sect VII, of *Poet in New York,* published in the *Revista de Occidente* (Madrid).

1931:
March   First public reading of *Poet in New York,* at the Residencia de Estudiantes in Madrid.

1932:   "Unsleeping City," from Sect. III, and "Girl Drowned in the Well," from Sect. VI, of *Poet in New York,* published in *Poesía espagnola: antología 1915-1931.* Selected by Gerardo Diego. Signo (Madrid).

1933:   "The King of Harlem," from Section II of *Poet in New York,* is published for the first time in *Los Cuatro Vientos* (Madrid) as "Ode to the King of Harlem."

1933:   The "Ode to Walt Whitman," from Section VIII, is published for the first time, in a limited edition in Mexico

1933:   Lorca arrives in Buenos Aires.
A public reading of *Poet in New York,* reported by A

fredo de la Guardia in *García Lorca: persona y creación* (Buenos Aires: Editorial Sur, 1941) as follows:

"With a few introductory words, Lorca summed up the poem which he thereafter proceeded to read. 'I bring you a bitter and living poetry to lash your eyes open.' Amplifying his statement, he went on to declare that it was not his intention to entertain his public, but to wrestle with them, cheek to jowl, to disturb them, belabor them, to fight them to a fall or be struck down in turn. He sketched in the gigantic city with four strokes: 'an extra-human architecture, a furious rhythm, geometry, and anguish. . . . The gothic edges ooze from the hearts of the long-buried dead and ascend coldly, beauty without roots or fulfilled longing, gracelessly confident, neither surpassing nor transcending, as spiritual architecture should, the inferior strivings of the architect.' Very briefly and expressively, he laid bare the solitude of the poet in New York in the presence of man's immense struggle with the thrust of the skyscrapers, under an indifferent sky; his intense solitude under the countless, immutable windows and the glitter of illuminated billboards of Broadway." According to de la Guardia, Lorca saw a Harlem inhabited by " 'slaves of all the inventions of the white man, and his machines, living in perpetual fear that they might one day unlearn the lighting of a gas stove or the handling of a car or the fastening of a starch-stiffened collar, or drive a fork through an eye.' He complained of the melancholy of the negro and his vain efforts to bury all traces of his race under a mask of pomade and cosmetics."

1934:
24 March Lorca leaves Argentina for Spain.

1935:   "Earth and Moon," a New York poem subsequently
March   omitted from the canon of *Poet in New York*, published
          in *El Tiempo Presente* (Madrid).

1935:   Lorca prepares the text of *Poet in New York* for publica-
August   tion by the Ediciones Arbol (*Cruz y Raya*), Madrid.
          It is characteristic of Lorca, however, that the poem as a
          whole went unpublished for the six-year interval between
          his return to Spain in 1930 and his death in 1936. The
          chronology of Lorca's written work, as biographers and
          bibliographers of the poet have ruefully pointed out, sel-
          dom coincides with the dates of his published works.
          Thus, the *Poema del cante jondo,* written between 1921
          and 1922, remained unpublished for ten years thereafter;

183

the *Canciones,* composed between 1921 and 1924, was not published until 1927; while a volume of early lyrics, completed in 1921, received posthumous publication in 1936. In the case of *Poet in New York,* considerations of a more compelling and conscientious nature may have joined to bring about an enforced interval of "silence." It is obvious, in the first place, that Lorca was increasingly preoccupied with the theater as playwright and producer during these years, both in his own country as co-director of the "La Barraca" group, and in Buenos Aires, where he was invited to assist in the production of his own plays and the traditional masterpieces of his country. There is reason to believe, moreover, that the misgivings which led him to suspend production of his surrealist play of the same period, *Así que pasen cinco años,* and abandon another piece in the same vein, induced Lorca to take stock of his style and method in the present poem and question the oneirical licenses of his manner. Certainly, in the dramas which follow between 1930 and 1936, the struggle between excess and austerity, the Real and the Super-real, the Muse and the *Duende,* was constant, and culminated in the open avowal of "photographic documentation" in the *Casa de Bernarda Alba.* Lorca's boast to assembled listeners at an informal reading of the play in 1936, according to Adolfo Salazar, was: "See! Not a drop of poetry! Reality! Realism!" And though the "black sounds" and the "gored Dionysian cry" of the *Duende* reverberate in the concluding act of *Bodas de sangre* and the elegy for Ignacio Sanchez Mejias, the open cadences and the hallucinated automatism of his surrealist manner were abandoned by the poet.

1935:
August (?)

First letter to Miguel Benítez Inglott in Barcelona, requesting the text of the poem *"Crucifixión"* for inclusion in *Poet in New York*:

I am typing up my New York book to give the printer month after next in October; I earnestly implore you to send me by return mail the poem *"Crucifixión,"* since you are the only one who has a copy and I am without one. Later on, I will inscribe it to you in the book . . . Miguel, do be good enough and kind enough to send on the poem. It is one of the finest to go into the book.

1935:

14 August Second letter to Miguel Benítez Inglott:

Some days ago I wrote you a letter begging you to send me my poem *"Crucifixión,"* now in your possession. Since I have had no answer, I am writing you again to remind you, begging you to let me have it since the poem is one of the most interesting in the book and I don't want it to be lost.

It is apparent, however, that *"Crucifixión"* was in fact lost, not once, but twice, to its custodian, Don Miguel Benítez, and for fifteen years to the canon of *Poet in New York*. It is listed by Rolfe Humphries as a poem intended by Lorca as the third poem of Section VII, but missing from his typescript of the manuscript and unavailable for inclusion in his 1940 edition. Subsequent Spanish texts of the poem both in Mexico and Buenos Aires, each professing to publish the poem "in full," do not include the poem and seem unaware of its omission. In the most recent one-volume edition of Lorca's collected works (Madrid: Aguilar, 1954), *"Crucifixión"* appears in an Appendix to the poem, rather than in the place reserved for it by the Humphries manuscript. According to Arturo del Hoyo, of Editorial Aguilar, there is extant a letter from Lorca removing it from the canon of this work and reserving it for publication in a subsequent book. The testimony of Don Miguel Benítez, however, makes it clear that the poet's "choice" was in reality the unhappy consequence of the absent-mindedness or the dereliction of a friend, and that no other course was open to Lorca at the time. In view of Lorca's emphatic insistence upon the importance of the poem to the scheme of his "New York book," I have preferred to restore it to the sequence suggested by Mr. Humphries, though Mr. Humphries' typescript, alas, is a far from redoubtable umpire.

185

1935:   "Nocturne of the Void," from Sect. VI of *Poet in New York,* published in *Caballo Verde Para la Poesía* (Madrid).

1935:

December Public reading of *Poet in New York* in Barcelona.

1936:

August (?) Lorca murdered in Granada by Franco *falangistas.*

1938:   "Ode to the King of Harlem" and "Ode to Walt Whitman" published in Volume VI of the "complete" works of Lorca (Buenos Aires: Editorial Losada).

1938:   Rolfe Humphries begins his English translation of *Poet in New York.*

1939:   "King of Harlem" and fragments of the "Ode to Walt Whitman" translated into English by Stephen Spender and J. L. Gili, with an Introduction by R. M. Nadal (London: The Dolphin; New York: Oxford University Press).

1940:   Bilingual edition of *Poet in New York,* in the Humphries translation, published by W. W. Norton, New York, from "typescript not always perfectly clear and at times declaring its own confusion." The volume contains an Introduction by José Bergamín (an abbreviated version of his preface to the Mexican edition of the poem), a Translator's Note, a Biographical Note by Herschel Brickell, and a selection from the "briefer songs" and "gypsy ballads" of Lorca. Three poems intended for inclusion by the poet in *Poet in New York* are declared missing: *"Tu infancia en Menton"* ("Your Childhood in Menton"), *"Amantes asesinados por una perdiz"* ("Lovers Slain By A Partridge"), and *"Crucifixión."*

1940:   First Spanish edition of *Poeta en Nueva York,* including the "missing" *"Tu infancia en Menton,"* published by Editorial Séneca (Ediciones Arbol) in Mexico City, 1940.

186

The volume contains an Appendix of textual variants ("Ode to the King of Harlem," "Abandoned Church," "Landscape of Vomiting Multitudes," "Double Poem of Lake Eden," "Death," "Nocturne of the Void," "Ruin," "Office and Denunciation," "Little Viennese Waltz"); four original drawings in color by the author; an elegy by Antonio Machado; and a Preface by José Bergamín, editor and director of the Ediciones Arbol (in exile).

The following note is signed with the initials of Editorial Séneca:

The original of *Poet in New York,* which we are keeping as a memorial of the book, Federico García Lorca placed in the hands of his friend, José Bergamín, for the Ediciones Arbol inaugurated in Spain by the publication, *Cruz y Raya.* It was the poet's particular wish that the first edition of this book appear at the discretion of the director of the Spanish publications of the Arbol imprint, to whom he had confided both the publication of all his dramatic works and the promise of his complete poems. Publication of Lorca (by *Cruz y Raya*) had already begun in Spain with the *Lament for Ignacio Sanchez Mejias* and the first volume of his plays, *Blood Wedding* (1935). Today, Ediciones Arbol, reappearing under the imprint of Editorial Séneca (Mexico) and directed by its original founder, carries out the poet's directive with the publication of his original manuscript until now never printed in its entirety. Only a handful of these poems published prior to his death and a few—a very few—published thereafter, will not be wholly new to readers of Federico García Lorca.

1942:   Spanish text of *Poeta en Nueva York,* based on the Mexican edition of 1940, published by Editorial Losada (Buenos Aires) as Volume VII of the *Obras completas.*

1948:   Guillermo Diaz-Plaja reprints the full text of *"Tierra y luna"* ("Earth and Moon," Appendices, p. 143) in his *Federico García Lorca: estudio crítico* (Buenos Aires: Editorial Guillermo Kraft Ltda.), with the following remarks:

Under the title *"Tierra y luna,"* the poem appeared separately in an otherwise ephemeral publication, *El Tiempo Presente* (Madrid, March, 1935). It is a work representative of his American phase. The dramatic clash between the instinctual and the rational—Life-Earth, Death-Moon—gives a Dionysian air to the poem that the poet signed from the backwoods of America—in the Cabin of Dum Kunium (*sic*), Vermont, August, 1929. The tone, the symbolism, and the movement of the poem itself, place it in the period of *Poet in New York* . . . There is nothing to differentiate this poem in subject matter or form from his New York compositions.

Though Vermonters will probably dismiss the allusion to the American backwoods (*"plena selva americana"*) as a neo-primitive regression to the world of Leatherstocking and Chateaubriand, there is every reason, including the ubiquitous place name of Brooklyn, to credit Dr. Diaz-Plaja's supposition and applaud his vigilance. *"Tierra y luna"* is a poem which falls into the orbit of *Poet in New York,* if not into its canon, and might very well appear among the poems in Section VI, reserved by the poet for his "poems of solitude in Vermont." In the absence of more positive confirmation, however, and in consideration of his sister's assurance that Lorca "did not have occasion to include the poem in *Poet in New York,* though it seems to belong with the book," I have placed it among the Appendices. It so appears in the one-volume edition of the Aguilar classics, along with a note by Arturo del Hoyo, declaring that "the poem doubtless belongs to the cycle of *Poet in New York.*"

1950:   *"Crucifixión,"* missing from all previous editions of *Poet in New York,* is published for the first time in a separate brochure limited to 500 copies by Imprenta Ortega, Las Palmas, under the supervision of Los Hermanos Millares Sall and Rafael Roca. The booklet contains introductory Notes by Miguel Benítez Inglott, dedicatory poems by Augustin and José Maria Millares Sall, photostats of the pencilled manuscript and two typewritten letters by Lorca, as well as the text of the poem itself, printed in full.

Don Miguel Benítez concludes his Notes with the extraordinary explanation:

Federico made me a present of the original pencil-script, on the occasion of his stay in Barcelona. I kept it, according to my custom, in a copy of one of his books. When he asked me for the manuscript—as the letters reproduced here testify—I could find it nowhere. When the civil war was at an end, I resumed my search for it eagerly. I had moved to Madrid during the first days of August (1936), leaving all my books in Barcelona. Not until the May of 1939 did I have access to them again, and one day, between the pages of the *Romancero gitano,* I discovered the manuscript, which is now a relic.

Later, in the Canary Islands, I mislaid it again by some odd chance: until I began to believe—Heaven forgive me!—that someone had made off with it. And then, another fine day, between the leaves of the very same *Romancero,* I had the pleasure of finding the precious manuscript that, more recently, since I know my own days to be numbered, I have passed on to another fine poet who shares my veneration for the memory of Federico and my admiration for his work—Augustin Millares Sall. For the same reasons, I have presented his brother, José María, also a genuine poet, with the original of *"Oficina y denuncia"* ["Office and Denunciation," re-titled "New York," Section VII, *Poet in New York*], and Rafael Roca, my good and learned friend, with *"Homenaje a Maupassant"* [re-titled *"Amantes asesinados por una perdiz,"* "Lovers Slain By A Partridge," Appendices, p. 152), a prose piece in typescript with extensive and important textual corrections by the author.

1950: *"Pequeño poema infinito"* ("Little Infinite Poem") appears for the first time, as an "unpublished poem from *Poet in New York,"* in a supplement to a volume of letters, *Cartas a sus amigos,* edited by Sebastián Gasch for Ediciones Cobalto (Barcelona). The volume contains, in addition to two drafts of the poem, letters to Sebastián Gasch, Guillermo de Torre, Ana Maria Dalí, Angel Ferrant, and Juan Guerrero, with a Preface by Gasch and 30 reproductions of photographs, autographs, and drawings by the poet.

Unlike *"Crucifixión,"* this poem is not listed by Humphries as a "missing" poem, nor is its "omission" noted by previous editors of *Poet in New York;* and its owner, Juan Guerrero, has not made known the basis for his assertion that it is an "unpublished poem from *Poet in New York."* Fortunately, the photostat of Lorca's letter of August 14, 1935 to Inglott offers a clue in the shape of a corroboratory postscript in the author's hand, asking

Don Miguel Benítez whether he has in his possession also "a poem called *'Pequeño poema infinito'?"* Its collocation with *"Crucifixión"* at a time when Lorca was "typing up his New York book" makes it seem likely that the poem was indeed intended for inclusion in that work, and that, like *"Crucifixión,"* it was a casualty of his friendly benefactions. Here again, I have followed the practise of the Aguilar edition of 1954 and included it in the Appendices, until, and in the event that, its place in the canon of the poem can be established.

1950:   *"Amantes asesinados por una perdiz"* ("Lovers Slain By A Partridge"), the third of the "missing" poems cited by Rolfe Humphries, is published for the first time in *Homenaje a Maupassant* ("Planas de Poesia" XI [Canary Islands: Las Palmas]). According to Juan Guerrero, the "poem" was first given to him for a little magazine initiated by Jorge Guillén and himself in 1926, but which never progressed beyond the galley-proof stage.

Examination reveals the "poem" to be a prose exercise in "surrealism"—or at best, a *poème en prose*—in the style of the fugitive pieces, *"Nadadora sumergida"* ("Swimmer Submerged") and *"Suicidio en Alejandria"* ("Suicide in Alexandria") written by Lorca in 1928 and translated in the Appendices (p. 148). Despite its inclusion among the "missing" poems of *Poet in New York* by Humphries, there is nothing whatever to suggest that it has any bearing, substantively, formally, or chronologically, on the plan and canon of that book. It would be surprising to discover that Sr. Guerrero is correct in assigning a date as early as 1926, since there is a letter from the poet (See Notes, p. 178) dating his first ventures in "my spiritualized new manner"—classified by him as *prose* and by his critics as surrealist poetry—to 1928. In either case, however, the dates would fix

"Amantes asesinados por una perdiz" well in advance of *Poet in New York.*

The piece is included in the Appendices, along with *"Nadadora sumergida"* and *"Suicidio en Alejandria"*— with which it can hardly be compared for gayety of invention—because it shows Lorca cumbrously at play with the rhetoric of surrealism, just as *Poet in New York* reveals him therapeutically at work in the plenum of the surreal, and helps to measure the gravity of his final achievement.

The English text follows corrected proof-sheets of the "1926" version supplied by Juan Guerrero, and is in many respects inferior to the Las Palmas version published as an appendix to the Aguilar edition of Lorca's collected works. For that very reason, however, I have included it here, as an early improvisation on a text subsequently clarified and emended by its author.

1954:   First complete edition of the *Obras completas* of Federico García Lorca to be published in Spain, in classic one-volume thin-paper format, by Editorial Aguilar, with an Introduction by Jorge Guillén. The canon of *Poet in New York* here exactly follows the order and the content of the first Mexican and Argentine editions of the poem, with all "missing" or conjectural poems assigned to the Appendix, as indicated.

1955:   Second printing of the *Obras completas* by Editorial Aguilar, with 171 additional pages of letters, prose sketches, lectures, articles, drawings, posthumously published verse, and newspaper interviews. The latter include two interviews with Lorca on the subject of *Poet in New York:* one entitled *"Estampa de Garcia Lorca"* ("Impression of Garcia Lorca") in the *Gaceta Literaria,* Madrid, 15 January 1931, by Gil Benumeya (See entry for 1930:

191

Summer, page 182); the other entitled " 'Iré a Santiago':
Poema de Nueva York en el cerebro de García Lorca"
(" 'I'll Go to Santiago': New York Poem in the Brain of
Garcia Lorca"), by L. Mendez Dominguez, in *Blanco y
Negro,* Madrid, No. 2177, 5 March 1933. A third piece,
reporting "A Lecture and Reading of Verse by Federico
García Lorca at the Residencia de Señoritas," and signed
with the initials of Victor de la Serna, is reprinted from
El Sol (Madrid) 17 March 1932, along with the text of
the "Son of Negroes in Cuba."

— B. B.